Vivaldi

H.C. ROBBINS LANDON

Vivaldi

VOICE OF THE BAROQUE

With 31 illustrations

THAMES AND HUDSON

Contents

꙰

To Wolf Erichson,
Europe's greatest music producer

PROLOGUE

The Rediscovery of Vivaldi

❧

In 1950, I happened to be in New York when the famous Cetra recording of *The Four Seasons* arrived at The Liberty Music Shop and a clerk put it on. The shoppers, myself included, stopped their own activities and started to listen, entranced, to this seductive music which had lain forgotten on library shelves for two hundred years.

The Vivaldi renaissance had begun. It was to continue until, in 1990, Nigel Kennedy's recording of *The Four Seasons* topped the bestseller lists in London for many months. *The Four Seasons*, in short, has become the most popular piece of classical music in the world, and it was to investigate this extraordinary phenomenon that I decided to write this present book. Pieces of music do not arrive at such an august position – one of solitary splendour which not even Mozart has managed to approach – without some reason. I considered that a new examination of Vivaldi's life and works might, perhaps, reveal the secret of this unprecedented success, particularly among young people. What was it about *The Four Seasons*, and indeed much of Vivaldi's other instrumental work, especially the famous *L'estro armonico* (Opus 3), that had so capitivated musicians of the stature of J.S. Bach, as well as generations of teenagers in five continents in the latter part of our century? Why did it sink into such utter oblivion, and by what stages was it rediscovered?

When Vivaldi died in 1741, in great poverty, in Vienna, he was already forgotten. His body was buried in as cheap a fashion as possible in a small cemetery outside the city walls. His grave, and even the cemetery itself, have long since disappeared. It is with a certain *frisson* that we immediately think of Mozart and his shameful end – also in an unmarked grave, his only company the five

7

other anonymous dead bodies and the quicklime poured over them to speed them on their way to dust. In fact for years it was not even known that Vivaldi had died in Vienna, so little was the importance attached to the once-celebrated violinist and composer.

For two hundred years, only musicologists and historians knew the name of Antonio Vivaldi. In the twentieth century, with the revival of interest in Baroque music, he began to acquire a few admirers. One of the most interesting was the American writer Ezra Pound, who lived in Rapallo and put on remarkable concerts of Vivaldi there. He had among his friends and pupils the American violinist Olga Rudge, still alive as I write (she is now eighty-five), who was one of the principal performers at the Rapallo concerts between 1933 and 1939. 'In 1936, at Pound's instigation, she catalogued the three hundred and nine Vivaldi instrumental pieces in manuscript in the National Library in Turin; and following this she became one of the leading figures in Vivaldi's twentieth-century revival, eventually accepting a position as Secretary of the Accademia Chigiana in Siena, where she founded, together with the Italian musicologist S.A. Luciani, the Centro di Studi Vivaldiani.'[1]

The first comprehensive, if small, festival devoted to the music of Vivaldi in modern times took place at a most inauspicious moment, in September 1939, in the Aula Magna of the University of Siena. On Saturday 16 September, Fernando Previtali conducted an orchestral concert that included a Symphony in C, the G minor Violin Concerto (with Pina Carmirelli) and the Concerto 'alla rustica', as well as an Aria from *La fida Ninfa*. The central portion was devoted to the Concerto in B minor for four violins and orchestra (Opus 3, No. 10), followed by Bach's transcription of it for four harpsichords, played on pianos – since there were not four harpsichords available (though they used a harpsichord continuo throughout).[2]

Sunday, 17 September, was the second concert devoted to chamber music, containing among other things three arias from the opera *Ercole sul Termodonte*, the Concerto 'La notte' in G minor (RV 439) for flute and orchestra, and the large-scale Serenata for two sopranos, tenor, oboe, bassoon, two hunting horns, strings, harpsichord continuo and chorus (RV 690).

On the following Monday there was another instrumental concert, which included a Symphony in G, the Concerto for two violins and orchestra in A minor (Opus 3, No. 8), several arias, the Concerto in F for two oboes, two hunting horns, solo violin, strings and harpsichord continuo, and Bach's transcription for organ of the Concerto in D minor (Opus 3, No. 11). On Tuesday, 19 September, the Teatro della Reale Accademia dei Rozzi staged Vivaldi's opera *L'Olimpiade*, certainly for the first time since it had been given in Venice at the Teatro San Angelo in the winter of 1734.

The first concert of sacred music took place on Wednesday, 20 September. It included the *Credo* (RV 591), the Motet (RV 631) for soprano 'O qui coeli' and the *Stabat Mater* (which would become famous), ending with the *Gloria* (RV 589), which was soon to become Vivaldi's most popular piece of sacred music.

The programme notes were models of scholarly accuracy: they listed all the editors of the various pieces, among whom were Alfred Einstein, Virgilio Mortari (for the opera) and in most instances the distinguished composer Alfredo Casella, who had devoted months to seeking out the original manuscripts and copies. They came from the Biblioteca Nazionale di Torino (Turin) in ten cases, but also from the Saxonian Landesbibliothek in Dresden, the Berlin State Library, the Biblioteca del Liceo Musicale in Bologna, the Library of Congress in Washington, the Bibliothèque du Conservatoire in Paris and the Bibliothèque Nationale in Paris.

It was a noble beginning to our Vivaldi revival, and it also encouraged the famous publishing house of G. Ricordi in Milan to start, two years after World War II, the publication of all the instrumental works of Vivaldi. Soon the Vivaldi publishing renaissance was to include, among the editors, another celebrated Italian composer, Gian Francesco Malipiero, from a patrician family of Vivaldi's place of birth, Venice. Malipiero had edited huge quantities of the music of Claudio Monteverdi, whose *opera omnia* he had supervised for Universal Edition in Vienna, and now he edited a substantial part of Vivaldi's *oeuvre*. A milestone in Vivaldi's popularity occurred in 1950, when Malipiero published, with Ricordi, the score and parts of *Il cimento dell'armonia e dell'invention*, Opus 8, of which the first four concertos were *The Four Seasons, Le Stagioni*. Malipiero's realization of the organ and/or harpsichord part was to an extent a masterpiece of nineteenth-century Romantic thinking, especially his arpeggios in the *Adagio molto* section of *Autumn* describing the sleeping drunkards; nowadays we prefer the eighteenth-century, mundane, continuo part; but when the first recording of *The Four Seasons* came out with the Italian gramophone firm of Cetra, they of course used Malipiero's new score. In this fashion *The Four Seasons* made its way, on many 78 r.p.m. shellac discs, to New York.

Today Vivaldi is a household name all over the world. There have been more than 150 complete records of *The Four Seasons* at present writing – and many scholars have ensured that new information about his life and music is presented in several series of annual (and occasional) publications. The first Collected Edition of his music, by Ricordi, is well on its way to completion. There are hundreds of recordings on CD of his music in expert performances, many on period instruments directed by leading conductors such as Nikolaus Harnoncourt, Christopher Hogwood and Trevor Pinnock.

But perhaps the most sensational discovery about Vivaldi since World War II has been the gradual publication, performance and recording of his church music – a wealth of magnificent *settecento* culture of which hardly anyone knew anything half a century before now. There is, indeed, a general feeling among many musicians that this part of the Red Priest's *oeuvre* may, when it is all known and published, not only equal but perhaps even surpass the glorious instrumental music that has made his reputation. The fate of Vivaldi's operas still, in a sense, hangs in the balance; and it remains to be seen if we will experience the same kind of operatic revival for Vivaldi that we have observed with Claudio Monteverdi and in recent years with Handel, Lully and Rameau.

I believe that Vivaldi's most popular works do indeed contain something hypnotically fascinating for millions of listeners; and what makes the situation even more piquant is that just as many works by Vivaldi, especially the operas – less the church music – seem to be of no interest to the twentieth-century ear whatever. This stratification is quite different in the case of Mozart, whose various kinds of music – opera, symphony, mass, quartet, trio, divertimento, piano concerto, violin concerto – are all equally popular.

I have occupied myself in a desultory way with Vivaldi since the 1950s when I published the first edition of the *Magnificat* edited from a manuscript at Osek Monastery in Bohemia. Later, in Venice, I did research in the Pietà and in the various archives – that of the Conservatory was largely uncatalogued when I was working there in 1953–54 – and, apart from concentrating on Haydn, I also found many interesting Vivaldi sources. Later, I studied the Turin manuscripts. My old friend the Austrian composer Karl-Heinz Füssl and I also examined the operas.

This biography is an attempt to present the latest knowledge about Vivaldi and his music to the general public. The time could hardly be more ripe. Fifty years ago we knew nothing of his life but the barest of outlines. Now, every year, new facts, documents and even autograph letters appear in bewildering profusion. In the late 1980s no fewer than *fifty-two* letters to Vivaldi from the Florentine impresario Marchese Luca Casimiro degli Albizzi, director of the Teatro alla Pergola in Florence, have come to light. Equally surprising, autograph letters from Vivaldi to the Duke of Mecklenburg-Strelitz, not hitherto a figure on the Vivaldian scene, were discovered in East Germany. On 6 December 1991, at a famous auction by Sotheby's in London (when a Beethoven autograph piano sonata fetched £1 million), an autograph letter by Vivaldi to Marquis Bentivoglio of 16 (or 26) November 1737 was bought by a New York private collector for £59,400. The market-place value of composers' autograph manuscripts (music and letters) is a perhaps vulgar but nevertheless secure way to evaluate their estimation in the public's eye.

Vivaldi's life was interesting and atypical, and many of his admirers might like to examine the sources for themselves. In this biography, therefore, I have tried to translate all known letters *by* Vivaldi, many for the first time complete in English, as well as to summarize those written to the composer. I have concentrated on certain aspects, and certain works, of the instrumental music that I considered to be of particular importance; and there is a whole chapter on the religious music, with details of a number of works that I believe to be of especial beauty. Some, such as the 'other' (i.e. less well-known) *Gloria* (RV 588), will be new to many people and I imagine that they will be as surprised and enchanted with them as I.

All the translations, except as noted below, are my own. Vivaldi's music is identified by the catalogue drawn up by Peter Ryom (*Ryom-*

Verzeichnis). There is, below, a list of acknowledgments of published sources (with translations, etc.). Here, I should like to thank *Maestro* Flavio Colusso (Rome), Mrs F.G. Morrill (Florence), Lisa Cox (Exeter), Albi Rosenthal (London and Oxford) and *I Tatti* (Florence) for help in assembling the sources. Dr Otto Biba (Vienna) and Dr Stephen Roe (London) kindly provided useful information. My wife Else Radant Landon made innumerable transcriptions of original Italian documents and assisted in difficult problems of translations, as did Mary Giuntoli (Buggiano, Italy), particularly as regards the Venetian dialect.

H. C. R. L.
Château de Foncoussières
Christmas 1991

(RV = *Ryom-Verzeichnis*, the concordance of Vivaldi's works by which his music is now identified. See Bibliography under 'Ryom, Peter').

I
Priest and Music Master

൙

The Venice into which Vivaldi was born, on 4 March 1678, was a great city that had passed its prime. No longer one of the leading powers of Europe, she was still rich, proud and famous. Visitors from every country flocked to her for her festivities, her art and above all her music.

Venice's ancient music tradition, ecclesiastical and secular, was markedly different from that of other Italian cities. In the first place, the liturgy in use at the Basilica San Marco was not the same as that in use in the rest of Catholic Europe; secondly, the processional and ceremonial music favoured by the Serenissima was a remarkable fusion of sacred and worldly. The Basilica itself was not the Cathedral, as many people must have imagined, but rather the private chapel of the Venetian government, rendered a liturgical centre not least because of the holy relics of Saint Mark himself. Since musical life in Venice was centred around, though of course not exclusively limited to, the Basilica, the acoustics of the building gave rise to a peculiar Venetian choral technique – the use of multiple choirs, or *cori spezzati*, situated in different places within the edifice. All this meant that Venice required composers 'in residence' to furnish church and state (here to be considered an entity) with the enormous amount of music required for the many holidays and feast days observed by the Republic. Gradually there arose a magnificent school of Venetian music which was very different from the rest of Italian music. The great names of the *scuola* have become part of our international musical heritage – Andrea Gabrieli (c. 1515–86), his even more brilliant nephew Giovanni (c. 1555–1612), Claudio Monteverdi (1567–1643) and his pupil Francesco Cavalli (1602–76). Giovanni Gabrieli's most celebrated pupil was the German Heinrich Schütz (1585–1672), who came to Venice in 1609 and published his first music there (nineteen Italian madrigals); he returned to Venice again in 1628, when he studied closely the new style which had since developed, especially the music of the 'ingenious Herr Claudio Monteverdi'.

In Monteverdi's time opera had come to Venice, and the old master's *L'incoronazione di Poppea* had been written for the newly established San Cassiano theatre in 1642, when he was seventy-five. If hitherto Venice had been world famous for its ecclesiastical/ceremonial music, with its grave dignity and massive, brassy sound, the focus now began to shift to opera, a trend also to be seen in the *oeuvre* of Monteverdi's pupil Cavalli, who is thought to have composed some forty-two operas.

The arrival of the eighteenth century to Venice was a blessing, marking the end of a century of wars, pestilence and universal suffering. As light follows darkness, the *settecento* followed the dark, evil *seicento*. The musical centre of Venice had shifted away from San Marco and the other great churches to the opera houses on the one hand and to the orphanages on the other, for both of which Vivaldi was to compose much of his most beautiful and lasting music.

Antonio Vivaldi's father, Giovanni Battista Vivaldi, was a barber but was also connected to his father's bakery trade; he soon became a professional musician, however, joining the orchestra of San Marco on 23 April 1685 – the starred year of the births of J.S. Bach, G.F. Handel and Domenico Scarlatti. Giovanni Battista (often abbreviated in Venice as 'Gianbattista') had the red hair which his son inherited. His entry in San Marco's pay list was 'Gio: Baptista Rossi' ('Rossi' = red-head)[1] and he soon received a rise in salary from fifteen to twenty-five ducats (21 August 1689) because of 'a major increase of new functions involving the use of orchestral instruments and organs.' Eleanor Selfridge-Field discovered that two other musicians at San Marco, a violinist and a cellist, also received these increases, suggesting the formation of a *concertino* group within the new *concerto grosso* form: the *concertino* consisted of two violins and cello (with or without continuo, i.e. harpsichord or organ) but was also used as a solo group, or string trio (for which composers were beginning to write); the *concertino* scoring sometimes appeared in larger pieces of church music, for instance, in Handel's Roman oratorio *La Resurrezione* (1708), where in the opening Sonata (i.e. Overture) we find solo violin and solo cello in the very Corellian *concertino*.

The entry of Vivaldi's birth in the register of San Giovanni in Bràgora was discovered only in 1962 (facsimiles of it are now sold in the church). His parents are recorded as 'Giovanni Battista Vivaldi, son of the late Augustin, instrumentalist [*Sonador*], and his wife Camilla Calicchio.' This baptism took place two months after the birth of Antonio Lucio (as he was registered): 'born on 4 March last, who was baptised at home, being in danger of death, by the midwife Madama Margarita Veronese, was today taken to the church and received the exorcisms and holy oils from me, Giacomo Fornaciere, parish priest, at which he was held by Signor Antonio Veccelio, son of the late Gerolemo, apothecary, at the sign of the dose in the same parish.'[2] The parents had been married on 6 August 1677, hence Antonio was either a premature child or conceived before wedlock: if premature, that may explain his sickly state at birth and later in life.

Antonio was one of many children – he had three sisters and two brothers – and they seem to have been a rowdy collection. One brother was banned from Venice in 1721 after a row at dawn following a raucous night, and another member of the family (probably a brother), Iseppo, was banned for five years for wounding a baker's boy in a brawl. Iseppo was identified by one of the witnesses, who said, à propos of that violent affair on 9 November 1728, 'Iseppo, non so il cognome, fratello de Prete rosso famoso che sona il violin' ('Iseppo, I don't know his surname, he's the brother of the famous red-haired Priest who plays the violin').[3]

Vivaldi is reported to have studied with the *maestro di cappella* at San Marco, Giovanni Legrenzi (1626–90), one of whose themes was immortalized by J.S. Bach in the so-called 'Legrenzi' Fugue (BWV 574).[4]

Certainly the precocious Antonio had already composed a piece of church music, *Laetatus*, the autograph of which (in the Turin Library) is dated 1691, a year after Legrenzi's death. Antonio is also reported to have studied violin with his father – this would have been natural – and to have been a member of the San Marco orchestra, even deputizing for his father when Giovanni Battista was absent from Venice during the years 1689–92.[5]

In spite of this precocious musical talent, he was destined, as the eldest son of a poor family, for the priesthood, where he might be expected to achieve more than would be possible in a more humble profession (even a richer family would have placed a younger son in the church). Hence, Vivaldi received the tonsure on 18 September 1693, aged fifteen and a half, from the Venetian patriarch, and on 19 September he became an Ostario (Porter), the first of the so-called minor orders. He had received instruction from priests at two local parishes, San Giovanni in Oleo and San Geminiano; he was obviously considered too weak to attend a seminary, and in the eighteenth century it was entirely 'possible to become a priest outside a seminary, as assistant to a minister to whom one was assigned ... during one's time of study and apprenticeship.'[6] His progress up to ordination may be charted from the Archivio Patriarcale in Venice as follows:[7]

Tonsure:	18 September 1693
Minor Orders	
Ostario (Porter)	19 September 1693
Lettore (Lector)	21 September 1694
Exorcista (Exorcist)	25 December 1695
Accolito (Acolyte)	21 September 1696
Holy Orders	
Subdiacone (Sub-Deacon)	4 April 1699
Diacone (Deacon)	18 September 1700
Sacerdote (Priest)	23 March 1703

The combination of a musical career with that of a priest was by no means unusual in the eighteenth century: another famous example is the Spaniard Padre Antonio Soler (1729–83), cathedral chapel master at the monastery of El Escorial near Madrid. Vivaldi's difficulty was that, because of his illness, which he later described as *strettezza di petto* (literally: tightness in the chest), he soon had to give up celebrating mass altogether.

Vivaldi in 1723 – 'il Prete Rosso
compositore di musica' – a slightly
malicious caricature by Pier Leone
Ghezzi, but in spite of that conveying
the most vivid impression of what he
must have been like.

(Left) *Vivaldi's baptismal entry in the register of S. Giovanni in Bràgora (below), 6 May 1678. A weakly child 'in danger of death', he had already been baptized at home shortly after his birth in March the same year.*

(Right) *A contemporary view of another Venetian church, S. Zaccaria, during the celebration of Easter.*

19

(Below) *The Ospedale della Pietà (the large building in the centre) on the Riva degli Schiavoni, where Vivaldi taught music for much of his life.* (Left) *The Piazzetta at one end of the Riva was the centre of Venetian social life in Vivaldi's time.*

(Above) *A concert in a Venetian house, the orchestra on the left, audience on the right.* (Left) *'The Singing Lesson' by Longhi, a world which Vivaldi would have known well.* (Above right) *Visitors to Venice commented on the freedom allowed to convent girls, and many Venetians found convents a useful venue for seeking a wife. The painting by Guardi shows the girls talking to their friends through the grille.* (Below right) *A concert given by orphanage girls: the violinists are in the front row of the balcony.*

A girl's choir singing behind the grille of a
convent church. This was the experience
that so excited Rousseau when he was in
Venice in 1744. (See p. 30)

Years later (16 November 1737) he writes, 'When I had barely been ordained a priest I said mass for a year or a little more. Then I discontinued saying it, having on three occasions had to leave the altar without completing it because of this ailment.'[8] Nowadays it is presumed that Vivaldi suffered from acute asthma.

There has been much speculation about what happened to Vivaldi between his becoming a deacon in September 1700 and March 1703, when he was ordained a priest: one year was the minimum time required by the church. It used to be suggested that he went to Rome to study with the great Arcangelo Corelli (1653–1713), music master to Cardinal Ottoboni, whose uniquely personal style finds many echoes in Vivaldi's early music; but as Kolneder has aptly pointed out,[9] Corelli's music was also published in Venice as well as Rome and therefore easily available to anyone in the lagoon city. Nor is there any evidence of Vivaldi's going to Turin to study with the violinist and composer G.B. Somis (1686–1763) or vice versa. In any case, the year he was ordained (1703) is also the first in which Vivaldi's presence as teacher at the Pietà is recorded.

The Ospedale della Pietà, to give the institution its full name, was one of four charitable organizations in Venice formed to receive girls who were orphaned for one reason or another (illegitimacy was a principal reason). Of these four, the Pietà was the most celebrated, not least because of the high standard of its musical performances. It was founded in 1346 and is situated on the Riva degli Schiavoni. The adjoining chapel was expanded after Vivaldi's death, but before you reach it, coming from St Mark's, the building on the left where the musical school of the Pietà existed is marked by a plaque. The girls formed not only the choir but also all the instrumentalists in the orchestra, and contemporary reports are unanimous in their praise for the girls' proficiency, vocal and instrumental.

Since the vocal parts of the music performed at the Pietà included tenors and basses, a great deal of speculation has been perhaps wasted on identifying the sources of these supposed male parts. In fact, recent research suggests that the girls themselves supplied the tenor and bass line. In a list of 4 December 1707 we find among the new entrants two sopranos, four contraltos, three tenors and one bass, of which one is specifically described as 'Paulina dal Tenor' and another 'Anneta del Basso'.[10]

In 1703, the *Maestro di Coro* at the Pietà was the successful Luccan composer Francesco Gasparini (1668–1727), whose music to *Hamlet* has been revived recently with great success. The governors of the Pietà met on 12 August 1703, and deliberated as follows:

New Music Teachers
To increase ever further the perfection of the orchestra [*Coro*] and to introduce more polish into its performances, in accordance with the wishes of Signor Gasparini, it is moved that teachers of the *viola*, the violin and the oboe be appointed by the Officers in charge of Music [*Deputati sopra il Coro*] at a salary that shall be deemed proper, and no great expense to this venerable institution, and that their services be retained for as long as believed necessary, their duties being laid down by this Congregation [Board of Governors].

> For the resolution ....8⎫
> Against..........................2⎬ carried[11]
> Abstentions ....1⎭

Shortly after that date, Vivaldi was engaged as violin teacher (September 1703) and by 17 August 1704 the governors were moved to grant him a rise in salary:

Since the sustained efforts of Don Antonio Vivaldi, the girls' violin teacher, have borne fruit, and since he has also rendered diligent assistance in the tuition of the *viola inglese*, which is considered by Their Excellencies [the Governors] part of his duties, it is moved that 40 ducats be added to his normal salary on account of his teaching of the *viole all'inglese*, making a total of 100 ducats per annum, so that he may be encouraged in his tasks, and for the greater profit of those girls.

> For ....9⎫
> Against..........................1⎬ carried[12]

About a year later – the actual date of the publication is variously given as between 1703 and 1705 – the Venetian firm of Sala issued Vivaldi's Opus 1, a set of trio sonatas for two violins and *violone* (double bass) or harpsichord, the existence of which was discovered by the late scholar and composer Gian Francesco Malipiero, who found the first violin part in the Venice Conservatory of Music. Opus I shows its dependence on Corelli's Sonatas Opus 5, even to including variations on the celebrated melody *La Follia* (*Les Folies d'Espagne*), a sarabande-like dance of hypnotic power and fascination, but Vivaldi already demonstrates his powers of rhythmic concentration and formal tightness which were to serve him so brilliantly. The depressingly conventional dedication was to Annibale, Count Gambara, a Venetian nobleman whose family came from Brescia:

My devotion, ambitious to make itself known to your Excellency, has suffered enough from the torments of desire. I confess that many times I restrained my ardour, mindful of your merit and mistrustful of my talent, but, no longer able to contain my ambition, I thought it proper to free it from its longing, since what was earlier a mere propensity had become a necessity. When considering whether to dedicate to Your Excellency the first fruits of my feeble efforts in the form of these sonatas, I realized that it was no longer in my power not to do so. Your lofty prerogatives took my judgement captive and rewarded my decision with the bounty of a Maecenas. I will not lose myself in the vast expanse of the glories of your most noble and excellent family, for I would not find my way out again, since they are so immense in greatness and number. Knowing that I possess no other adornments than those of my feebleness, I have sought the patronage of a great man, who can not only protect me from the tongues of Aristarchuses [pedants – named after a grammarian of the second century BC], and in whose shade my labours – perhaps when maligned by critics, who in these times like to flaunt their impertinences – can enjoy a safe refuge, but can also perform these flaccid harmonies, which with so much humility I dedicate to Your Excellency. May your exalted generosity then deign to accept in respectful tribute these first, most humble products of my labours, and meanwhile grant me the honour of declaring myself:

the most humble, devoted and obliged servant of Your Excellency,

D. Antonio Vivaldi[13]

At the Pietà, Vivaldi's duties seem to have been numerous and varied. By the time he became music master the Ospedale contained 1,000 persons; the girls were divided into two groups: the *figlie di coro*, those who specifically studied music and were maintained by the Serenissima at a cost of some one hundred lire a head; and the *figlie di commun*, the non-musicians, who received a general education. The élite musicians were in a special class and were called the *privileggiate del coro*, and they were the ones who received offers of marriage and what we would call 'publicity.' The girls were referred to by their Christian names, e.g., 'Anna Maria of the Ospedaletto,' or, if they were the teachers, by the title of 'Maestra,' e.g., 'Maestra Lucretia della Viola, Maestra Cattarina dal Cornetto, Maestra Silvia dal Violino, Maestra Luciana Organista.' The Pietà looked after them, sent them on holiday if they seemed poorly; it provided 'Maestra Michieletta del Violino' with a basket of wood each week for eight months. The standard of the musicians was extraordinarily high and all the foreign visitors were in raptures over their abilities on all known instruments, even the kettledrums. (The authorities were rather anxious to get rid of a timpani teacher once the girls had learned how to play the instrument.) In 1745 the choir contained eighteen singers and eight string players with two organists, but there were fourteen *iniziate* as assistants – a total of about forty.[14]

President Charles de Brosses, whose eye-witness reports of daily life in Venice at this period are invaluable, reports that the orchestra of the Pietà had *le premier coup d'archet*, of which Mozart so sarcastically speaks as being a Parisian speciality, and so falsely boasted of at the Paris Opéra.

Northern visitors were rather shocked at the easy-going appearance and manners of the girls and nuns. Edward Wright[15] noted that

On their feast-days the door of their convent is flung open, and they stand in crowds at the entrance, where I observed them talking to their acquaintance with great freedom. Nor do these noble vestals at any time confine themselves to such close restrictions as others of their order are obliged to do. Those I saw at the Celestia were dressed in white; no veil over their faces; a small transparent black covering goes round their shoulders;

their heads were very prettily dressed; a sort of small thin coif went round the crown, and came under the chin; their hair was seen at the forehead, and nape of the neck: the covering on their neck and breast was so thin, that 'twas next to nothing at all ...

Infants are received into these hospitals – into the Incurabili (originally destined to another use) not without a sum given with them, into the Pietà, and the other two, as I take it, without any.

Those who would choose for a wife one that has not been acquainted with the world go to these places to look for them, and they generally take all the care they can, they shall be as little acquainted with the world afterwards.

Those put into the Pietà are generally bastards. There are a prodigious number of children taken care of in this hospital; they say they amount sometimes to at least six thousand, and that before the erection of this charity multitudes used to be found which had been thrown into the canals of the city. Every Sunday and holiday there is a performance of music in the chapels of these hospitals, vocal and instrumental, performed by the young women of the place, who are set in a gallery above and, though not professed, are hid from any distinct view of those below by a lattice of ironwork. The organ parts, as well of those of other instruments, are all performed by the young women. They have a eunuch for their master, and he composes their music. Their performance is surprisingly good, and many excellent voices are among them. And this is all the more amusing since their persons are concealed from view.

Vivaldi as a eunuch might not, perhaps, have been the favourite description of his condition. Alan Kendall quotes an amusing source on this subject, François Misson, in a letter of 14 February 1688:[16] 'They have found a means to accommodate the affair, and have concluded that a priest fitted for musick may exercise the priesthood as well as another; provided he hath his *necessities*, or, if you will, his *superfluities* in his pocket.' Presumably Wright considered that the former had become the latter in the case of Vivaldi at the Pietà.

President de Brosses, who was writing in August 1739 from Venice, notes that the ladies were now using gondolas to receive their lovers, and continues:[17]

This current practice of the ladies has much diminished the profits of the nuns, who were previously in the possession of *galanterie*. Even so, there are still a good number of them who come out of it today with distinction, I might say with emulation, since, even as I talk to you, there is a furious dispute amongst three convents of the city to decide which will have the advantage of giving a mistress to the new nuncio who has just arrived. In truth, it would be towards the nuns that I would turn most willingly if I had to stay here for long. All those that I have seen at Mass, through the grille, talking the whole of the time and laughing together, have seemed pretty to me and got up in such a way to set off their beauty. They have a charming little hair-style, a simple habit but, of course, almost entirely white, which uncovers their shoulders and throat no more nor less than the Roman costumes of our actresses ...

The transcendent music is that of the asylums. There are four of them, made up of illegitimate and orphaned girls and those whose parents are not in a position to raise them. They are brought up at the expense of the state and trained solely to excel in music. Moreover, they sing like angels and play the violin, the flute, the organ, the oboe, the cello, and the bassoon; in short, there is no instrument, however unwieldy, that can frighten them. They are cloistered like nuns. It is they alone who perform, and about forty girls take part in each concert. I vow to you that there is nothing so diverting as the sight of a young and pretty nun in a white habit, with a bunch of pomegranate blossoms over her ear, conducting the orchestra and beating time with all the grace and precision imaginable.

We might conclude with Rousseau's description, in his *Confessions*, of his experiences with the *figlie*. He writes:[18]

Music of a kind that is very superior in my opinion to that of the operas and that has not its equal throughout Italy or perhaps the world is that of the *scuole* ... Every Sunday at the church of each of these four *scuole* during vespers, motets for a large chorus with a large orchestra, which are composed and directed by the greatest masters in Italy, are performed in barred-off galleries solely by girls, of whom the oldest is not twenty years of ago. I can conceive of nothing as voluptuous, as moving as this music ... The church [I Mendicanti] is always full of music lovers; even the singers from the Venetian opera come so as to develop genuine taste in singing based on these excellent models. What grieved me was those accursed grills, which allowed only tones to go through and concealed the angels of loveliness of whom they were worthy. I talked of nothing else. One day I was speaking of it at M. le Blond's. 'If you are so curious,' he said to me, 'to see these little girls, I can easily satisfy you. I am one of the administrators of the house, and I invite you to take a snack with them.' I did not leave him in peace until he had kept his promise. When going into the room that contained these coveted beauties, I felt a tremor of love such as I never experienced before. M. le Blond introduced me to one after another of those famous singers whose voices and names were all that were known to me. 'Come, Sophie,' – she was horrible. 'Come, Cattina,' – she was blind in one eye. 'Come, Bettina,' – the smallpox had disfigured her. Scarcely one was without some considerable blemish. The inhuman wretch le Blond laughed at my bitter surprise. Two or three, however, looked tolerable; they sang only in the choruses. I was desolate. During the snack, when we teased them, they made merry. Ugliness does not exclude charms, and I found some in them. I said to myself that one cannot sing thus without soul; they have that. Finally, my way of looking at them changed so much that I left nearly in love with all these ugly girls.

Vivaldi's Opus 2 was published in Venice by Antonio Bortoli: it consisted of twelve sonatas for violin and harpsichord and its appearance coincided with the sudden arrival of King Frederick IV of Denmark and Norway who, in the fashion of the time, was travelling incognito, as the Duke of Olemborg. He arrived on 29 December 1708 and the next day, a Sunday, he was at the Pietà:

His majesty appeared at the Pietà at 11 o'clock after receiving ambassadors from Savoy, to hear the girls singing and playing instruments under the direction of the master [Vivaldi, it would seem] who was occupying the rostrum in the absence of

Gasparini. Great was the applause for the Credo and Agnus Dei which were performed with instruments, and afterwards there was a concert very much to his taste, as befitted him.[19]

Vivaldi was able to dedicate his new music to King Frederick IV – the wording was another characteristically fawning note:[20]

Dedication to King Frederic IV of Denmark and Norway
Sire,

Enviable is the fate of a humble heart if it is forced, when it meets a sovereign great by birth, but even greater by virtue, to ensure the multiplicity of his tributes, whatever they are. That truth obliges my intellect to reflect upon the heroic spirit of Your Majesty, so well known to the world, and it gives me great confidence to offer you my abasement which in real consideration of my nothingness could not in any way be more diminished.

Fate could do no more for you than elevate you to such eminence, majesty and might. But this height does not help the one so far below you; therefore you descended from the throne and your modesty removed the embarrassment of your high position, enabling you to console the one kneeling in front of you, who confesses to be unworthy of even kissing the lowest step of your throne.

Welcome therefore, O great King, not the offer which is in no proportion to your person, but consider the heart that brings it. Because, if the heart can give value to that which is low and has no importance, you can not avert your eye from that little offering which comes from a mind which cherishes with humble devotion the wish also to be esteemed; and in my desire to consider myself Your Majesty's most humble, devoted and obedient servant,

                                              Antonio Vivaldi

The title page lists Vivaldi's position as 'Musico di Violino, e Maestro de' Concerti del Pio Ospedale/della Pietà di Venezia', and the print is dated 1709 (copy in the Estense Collection, Vienna).

It would have seemed that Vivaldi's position in Venetian musical life, and as music master (or *maestro de' concerti*) at the Pietà, was unassailable. His contract with the Ospedale was renewed, year after year, but an astute observer could see that all was not well with the governors' opinion of their already famous composer-in-residence. In 1707 the voting was six to three, but in 1709 the catastrophe happened: at the ballot on 24 February seven voted to keep him and six – a very ominous minority – were against. Another vote was called for and someone switched sides – and Vivaldi's career at the Pietà was finished – at least *pro tempore*.

No one really knows how this extraordinary state of affairs came about. Obviously Vivaldi, now a prominent figure in the artistic society of Venice, was making not only friends and admirers, but enemies. But why matters came to a head in the middle of Carnival time in Venice remains a matter of speculation. Certainly Vivaldi was making music all over the town, at private concerts with the French Ambassador (1705), for the Imperial Ambassador during Carnival 1707–8, and no doubt for many other unrecorded events. If 1709 was a bleak year for Vivaldi, it was otherwise a brilliant year for the history of music in Venice: at Christmas time, the German composer George Frideric Handel, fresh from triumphs in Rome, Naples and Florence, and armed with protection from the highest circles of the Catholic Church – rumour had it that Handel had been very tempted to join the Church –, arrived in Venice to stage a new opera, *Agrippina*. It was always imagined that this extraordinary event passed Vivaldi by; but it seems that the Venetian composer was more involved with *Agrippina* than we used to think, and it is to this story of Handel's triumph that we must now turn.

II

A Career in Opera

𝕒

Handel arrived in Venice sometime during 1709. His biographer
Mainwaring chronicles that 'Venice was his next resort. He
was first discovered there at a Masquerade, while he was playing on
a harpsichord in his visor. [Domenico] Scarlatti happened to be
there, and affirmed that it could be no one but the famous Saxon, or
the devil ...'.[1]

The wording tells us that Handel must have been there during
Carnival time. At Epiphany in 1709, Venice and the lagoons were
plunged into freezing weather. The canals froze over. Our visitor
from the North, Frederick IV, was accused of importing the
intemperate weather. The incognito king went to the Pietà a second
time and had to leave early to attend a grand ball at the Foscarini
Palace. The King opened the festivities, dancing with the *procuratessa* Mocenigo, and then with Caterina Querini, a celebrated
beauty, 'whose riches were the least of her advantages.' Caterina's
necklace of pearls broke and the King stooped to collect them. Was
this the occasion, perhaps, when the equally incognito Handel
surprised Scarlatti and the King from the far North?[2]

Frozen Venice fascinated everybody: you could journey on the
ice from Mestre to San Marco, and carriages could cross the lagoons
with impunity. It was in the midst of this glacial atmosphere that
Vivaldi lost his job and Handel arrived with a libretto from his
patron at Naples, Cardinal Vincenzo Grimani, Viceroy and of
ancient Venetian lineage. Naturally, the libretto – destined for the
Teatro San Giovanni Crisostomo (which had been shut up for longer
than anyone could remember) – had to be passed by the censor, who
was in this case none other than the Grand Inquisitor himself,
Raimondo Pasquali. The document reads:

The undersigned declares solemnly to have read and approved according to the viewpoint of the Catholic Religion the book entitled l'Agrippina dramma per musica to be performed at the Teatro S. Gio Grisostomo [sic] of the signori Grimani, the autumn of the year 1709. Words by Cardinal His Eminence Vincenzo Grimani, noble Venetian.[3]

To this was added a MS. postscript, perhaps autograph, by Pasquali, 'The reformers know well the worth of His Eminence Card. Vincenzo Grimani, author of the drama which is to be present with the music of Giov. [*recte:* Giorgio] Haendel for the first time and by no means unknown ...'[4]

And now we find Vivaldi's name linked to *Agrippina*. In 1715 a pasticcio was produced called *Nerone fatto Cesare*, based on an older opera of the same name by Perti performed in 1693 at the Teatro San Samuele. This pasticcio included music by at least half-a-dozen composers, including Vivaldi with no fewer than twelve numbers. For this 1715 version of *Nerone* the censor was Giovanni Antonio Cattaneo, 'deputato alla Revision,' who noted that 'there was nothing against the principles and good customs' in the libretto, with the curious addition: 'The singers are the same who sang in *Agrippina* with Marietta from the Pietà.' Now it used to be thought that Handel's *Agrippina* must have been the work to which the censor referred; but it turns out that (1) there was an opera entitled *Agrippina* in the 1715 season; (2) it was very likely an earlier version of *Nerone fatto Cesare*. Johann Friedrich Uffenbach, a German visitor, heard both operas in 1715 and preferred the later version.[5] (Interesting to note that the orphanage girls were allowed to sing in opera at all. And that the fact was actually registered by the official censor of the Holy Inquisition.) Apropos the Vivaldi family and the Venetian theatres, the Italian scholar Remo Giazotto, to whom Vivaldians owe so much, discovered a fascinating document of 26 March 1710 – during the 'reign' of *Agrippina* – of the Teatro San Angelo in Venice, listing among the debtors Vivaldi's acquaintance Francesco Santurini, 'administrator of the designs in said theatre' and further down, 'Vivaldi Giovan Battista sonator di violino del ditto theatro ...'.[6]

History does not tell us why the theatre owed father Vivaldi money, but it does list him as closely involved with the San Angelo theatre as violinist. It also suggests that Antonio Vivaldi must have been increasingly drawn to the theatre, especially now since he lost his prestigious position with the Pietà. We have no idea whether Vivaldi met Handel, but it would be most unlikely that he did not, and repeatedly. Certainly the spectacular success of *Agrippina* – Vivaldi could not know how much was borrowed from earlier works in Rome and Florence – with its twenty-seven performances in Venice and its immediate transference to other theatres, Italian and abroad, must have indicated to Vivaldi that true success in the music world was not with the *figlie* of the Pietà but on the stages of the now flourishing opera houses. Certainly the delightful tunes of works like *Agrippina* were conquering even the halls of the ospedali and the churches of the Serenissima. C. Freschot, writing from Venice in 1709, had this to say about the situation:

> I do not know whether it is to cheer the saints' days up even more and for the special satisfaction of those who only go to church as they go to the theatres, that they scarcely ever fail in this noisy music to mingle the same arias that one has heard at the operas, and which have pleased more, and that with no scandal to the favour of the words which one changes and which, instead of expressing, for example, the loves of Pyramus and Thisbe, say something of the life of the saint whose feast day it is.[7]

Vivaldi remained outside the Pietà, at least officially, until 27 September 1711. Then, in the governors' minutes of the orphanage, we read:

> Realising the necessity of securing ever better instrumental tuition for the girls studying music in order to increase the reputation of this pious establishment, the post of violin master being vacant, we move that Don Antonio Vivaldi be appointed violin master at an annual salary of 60 ducats, this governing body being certain that he will exercise his talent to the utmost in the good service of this pious establishment, and for the greater profit of those girls.

$$
\left.\begin{array}{lr}
\text{Abstentions} \dots\dots\dots\dots\dots & 0 \\
\text{Against} \dots\dots\dots\dots\dots\dots & 0 \\
\text{In favour} \dots\dots\dots\dots\dots & 11
\end{array}\right\} \quad \text{carried[8]}
$$

Vivaldi's position was confirmed in 1712 and 1713. But why then had he been blackballed in 1709? It is all very mysterious and one feels the heavy hand of Venetian intrigue lurking behind much of these twistings and turnings. In 1713, Francesco Gasparini obtained sick leave for six months, but it seems clear that he never intended to return at all. Gasparini had enjoyed a very considerable success with operas in Venice, of which he had written no fewer than twenty-six between 1702 and 1713. At the same time he had composed nine oratorios, most for the Pietà. In 1713, when he was called on to write an opera each for Milan and Mantua, he had asked for a leave of one month 'à motivo dei suoi premurosi affari,' but when he asked for the six months it was 'à motivo de ricuperarsi dalle indisposizioni da quali resta aggravato.' It may be that the climate of Venice, which is humid and cold in the winter and humid and hot in the summer, really did not agree with him. The governors agreed, 'purché il maestro garantisca di provvedere anche fuori Venezia all'invio di composizioni nuove per le varie ricorrenze festive'; in other words he agreed to supply the Pietà with compositions for the various church feasts even when away from Venice.

Gasparini went from Venice to Città di Castello im Umbria and, three years later, on to Rome as *maestro di cappella* of Prince Ruspoli. The governors of the Pietà, 'stante l'absenza da questa Città del Signor Francesco Gasparini Maestro Attuale' (in view of the absence from this city of the present *maestro*, Francesco Gasparini), appointed Pietro Dall'Olio as a temporary director on 11 June 1713. He hardly lasted nine months. There was another interval during which it seems that the composition of new church music was more and more entrusted to Vivaldi. In a memorandum of 6 July 1710, the governors had listed the works they expected from their *maestro*: 'two new Mass and Vespers settings annually [one for Easter and the other for the feast of the Visitation of the Blessed Virgin, to whom the Pietà was dedicated]; at least two motets every month; occasional compositions as required for funerals, the offices of Holy Week, etc.'[9]

On 30 April 1713, the governors at the Pietà allowed Vivaldi a month's leave of absence 'all'impiego delle sue virtuose applicazioni,' and in this case the 'applications' were to permit the composer to journey to Vicenza to supervise the production of his first opera, *Ottone in Villa*, during the month of May.

The governors were altogether very satisfied with Vivaldi, and expressed themselves in no uncertain terms in a motion discussed on 2 June 1715:

This pious congregation [the governors] having noted from the petition of the Reverend Don Antonio Vivaldi, violin master in this pious establishment, and the deposition of the Officers in charge of Music just read out, the acknowledged services and well-rewarded labours performed by him, not only in the successful and universally approved teaching of musical instruments to the girls, but also the excellent musical compositions supplied after the departure of the above-mentioned *maestro* Gasparini – a complete Mass, a Vespers, an oratorio, over 30 motets and other works – and seeing fit in its generosity to give him a token of its gratitude and recompense him in part for these services outside his normal duties, resolves that a single payment of 50 ducats be made to him from our exchequer in appreciation of his efforts and special contributions. And may this reward also stimulate him to make further contributions and to perfect still more the performing abilities of the girls of this our orchestra, so necessary to the musical standards and the good reputation of this our chapel.

Abstentions 0
Against .... 2 } carried[10]
In favour 10

Opera had started its life in Florence as an attempt to revive the lost tradition of Greek drama. Naturally, the first opera productions were entirely supported by various noble houses, such as the Medici in Florence and the Gonzagas in Mantua, where Monteverdi had made operatic history with his production of *Orfeo* for the Carnival season of 1607.

By the time Vivaldi arrived on the operatic scene, Venice had become a centre of the art. Even in Monteverdi's old age, commercial operatic houses had begun to open in the city, and the late flowering of Monteverdi's operatic output, *L'incoronazione di Poppea*, had been put together for a commercial operatic venture in Venice in 1642, a year before the composer's death. The proprietor of these commercial opera houses was usually a noble or several nobles, such as the members of the Grimani family, whose domination extended to no fewer than three theatres – Santi Giovanni e Paolo, San Giovanni Crisostomo and San Samuele. The actual management was entrusted to a professional director or an impresario, in which role we shall later see Vivaldi.

Vivaldi's operas were *terra incognita* for most musicians even twenty-five years ago: there was no proper catalogue of them and no one could imagine if they were stageworthy or not: the history of the Siena performance of *L'Olimpiade* in 1939 (see above) was too long past and had, in any case, hardly created a sensation. So, when my publishers, the Universal Edition of Vienna, suggested a thorough investigation of Vivaldi's operas by myself and by my colleague, the late Karl-Heinz Füssl, I welcomed the idea whole-heartedly. I had happily collaborated with Füssl on many musical projects, including Vivaldi – his *Magnificat*, for instance, of which I had found a manuscript in the Monastery of Osek in Czechoslovakia in 1959 and which the Universal Edition subsequently published: I had discussed the grave textual problems with Füssl, who was not only a composer but also a great connoisseur of *settecento* music.

In those days, the Fondazione Cini on the island of San Giorgio in Venice was engaged in photographing the whole corpus of Vivaldi manuscripts, largely from the great collection in the University Library of Turin; and since we were collaborating with the Fondazione in many other projects (the Gabrieli edition of the late Denis Arnold), it was natural that we turned to them with our new Vivaldi proposal. The doyen of Vivaldi (and Monteverdi) scholarship, Gian Francesco Malipiero, went with us: he was sceptical. 'They are full of extraordinary beautiful music,' he said to us, 'but I simply cannot imagine how modern, twentieth-century audiences could put up with three hours of static, non-dramatic music like that.' We did not believe him: we had just started to revive Haydn's operas, and Carlo Maria Giulini's performance of *Il mondo della luna* at the Holland Festival, and subsequently at Aix-en-Provence, had proved to be the triumph of 1959.

So, in 1961, we embarked on our quest for Vivaldi's operas with high hopes. An extraordinary monk, Don Cisilinò, helped us: he brought out one opera after another from the Turin Library. We took them into the courtyard and studied them with fascination. But as we examined these autographs and authentic copies, page by page, it began to dawn on us that despite their extraordinary beauties, they were literally of another age and time, and it seemed to us very unlikely that we could effect a Vivaldi opera renaissance as we were in the successful process of doing with Haydn's stage works. Malipiero came to see us after ten days: he put his hand on our shoulders as Füssl and I were working at a table in the Venetian sunlight. 'Well, which one will you start with?' We sat in silence. 'What, giving up already?' I explained what our reactions had been. Sorrowfully, we shelved the project. Even with the spectacular arrival of Marilyn Horne on the Vivaldi operatic scene, it is doubtful if audiences of the 1990s are going to adopt Vivaldi operas in the same fashion as they have embraced *The Four Seasons* and *L'estro armonico*. If future history should prove us wrong, we will be the first to applaud.

In 1739, after Vivaldi had stopped producing operas, he reckoned that he had written ninety-four of them, which of course meant that, considering his professional career as a whole, he must have seen himself as primarily a composer of operas (see Appendix I). Actually, we are missing some two dozen of these operas, and it must be said, moreover, that Vivaldi was obviously including pasticcios and works by other composers which he arranged and produced. But even with our present knowledge, it must be obvious that a large part of Vivaldi's waking thoughts were devoted to opera; and it is therefore a rather grim irony of fate that this is the one aspect of his multi-faceted career which arouses little or no interest in the twentieth-century listener. No doubt we do Vivaldi a grave injustice: for years we did Handel the same injustice; yet even now, despite the fervent pleas of Winton Dean, it is not Handel the opera composer who has gripped the minds and hearts of men and women all over the world, but Handel the composer of oratorios, church music, orchestral music and chamber music. No doubt a large part of Handel's stupendous abilities went into operas, but that is not, nevertheless, the aspect of his towering personality by which most people remember him. It is for the same reasons, cruel but irreversible, that J.A. Hasse's music is forgotten and doomed to oblivion: if Hasse had written fascinating instrumental music, perhaps he would be as popular as Handel or Vivaldi; but he did not. Hasse was a fantastically successful contemporary of Vivaldi's: he lived from 1699 to 1783 and, when he died in Venice after a hugely profitable career in Italy with his famous wife as his principal soprano he was an important figure in the history of music – but only that. Even the late Renato Fasano's attempts to resuscitate *settecento* Italian opera – beginning with a brilliant series of performances and a recording of Paisiello's *Il barbiere di Siviglia* in the 1960s – must be accounted a failure – though a very noble one. Perhaps the twenty-first century will change all that: but at the moment it is almost impossible to stage these forgotten eighteenth-century Italian operas, for all their manifest beauties and charm. Why this should be so must remain a matter of speculation for musicologists and social historians.

III

'L'Estro Armonico'

In 1686, one year after Bach's birth, a Frenchman from Caen emigrated to Amsterdam and in 1695, after serving as an apprentice to two other firms, founded a music publishing house in his own name, Estienne Roger. He included his wife in the business and also his affairs-manager, and both were sometimes included on the title pages, as was Estienne's eldest daughter Jeanne. A second daughter married Michel-Charles Le Cène and took over the business after Estienne's death in 1722.

It is not known how Vivaldi came into contact with Roger, but it would seem that it was about 1711 that the Amsterdam firm issued the first published concertos by Vivaldi, Opus 3, *L'estro armonico*. *L'estro = oestrus*, which means, variously, sting, fancy, 'stimulus, vehement impulse, frenzy', according to the O.E.D. It embraced a set of twelve magnificent concertos for sometimes extremely odd combinations of instruments. It was, says the Vivaldi scholar Michael Talbot,[1] 'perhaps the most influential collection of instrumental music to appear during the whole of the eighteenth century' – a claim which is certainly not exaggerated. Obviously this series contains a selection of Vivaldi's concertos composed over a period of years, probably for the Pietà, but also for his own use, though the many multiple concertos suggest team-work of a Pietà-like organization and significance. Some require four solo violins. In 1715 the concertos were reprinted by the London firm of Walsh and Hare, and by 1717 Roger was obliged to reprint.[2]

It is undoubtedly significant that Roger also published the other most remarkable set of Italian concerti grossi in 1714 (three years after Vivaldi's Opus 3): Arcangelo Corelli's Opus 6, the classic, noble examples of their kind (including the deeply loved 'Christmas

Concerto', the eighth number of the set of twelve): these too had been composed variously before their collection and publication in Amsterdam. And without these two there would probably not have been the third greatest set of such works to have been written: Handel's Opus 6, composed in 1739 and published by John Walsh in October of that same year.[3]

It was not only the outward form, so original and different, of Vivaldi's *L'estro armonico* which fascinated and enthralled musicians all over Europe but the intensely personal style – the 'Vivaldi style' *par excellence*, with its wiry, nervous sound and that intense concentration of rhythmic designs which, once experienced, are literally unforgettable.

Among the many musicians who were spellbound by the *Estro armonico* was Johann Sebastian Bach, in far-away Saxony, who made six arrangements of works from the set for his own benefit and probably for teaching purposes or for performance by himself and his sons in the Bach-Telemann coffee-house concerts given on Fridays in Leipzig.[4] Two were for solo harpsichord, three for solo organ and one for four harpsichords and orchestra.

There is an enormous difference between the gravely beautiful Concerti Grossi Opus 6 by Corelli and those by Vivaldi. In some respects it is rather like Haydn (= Corelli) and Mozart (= Vivaldi). There is a certain stately impersonality in Corelli's music which inevitably pales before the torrent of emotions unleashed in 'The Harmonious Fancy' – just consider the impassioned beginning of Vivaldi's Opus 3 No. 11 in D minor, with those swooping canonic imitations in the two solo violins (*violini concertanti*) which continue, bar after bar, like some irresistible act of nature. It is unlike anything ever written or at least published before. After the sudden arrival of the solo violoncello the music swerves into an *Adagio e spiccato*, three bars rather like a slow introduction which, indeed, they prove to be, leading to a fugue which is as elaborate and on as grand a scale as many a fugue in J.S. Bach. This kind of intensely personal music will be echoed, seventy years later, in Mozart's D minor Piano Concerto No. 20, K. 466, whose passionate accents were as new to Vienna in 1785 as Vivaldi was new to Amsterdam in 1711. There is an inner tension in all this Vivaldian music which, perhaps unfairly, makes Corelli seem slightly tame –

though such a movement as the pastoral finale to the Christmas Concerto from Corelli's Opus 6 rises to heights of classical beauty and tenderness which remind us that this music was immediately, and rightly, regarded as the touchstone of the concerto grosso form.

What can explain the immediate and (in the eighteenth century) lasting success of *L'estro armonico*? It was, of course, not any one element. Rather it was the freshness, the vigour, the variety and, in the slow movements, the mysterious tenderness that captivated men's minds. It was also the sheer energy of the rhythms, often in combination with each other, which musicians and the general public found riveting. Almost every concerto has its share. If we take the beginning of Opus 3, No. 10, the Concerto for four *violini concertanti*, four orchestral violins, two violas, *violoncello concertante*, orchestral violoncelli, double basses and harpsichord, we find right at the outset an almost bewildering series of forceful rhythms. First is the hypnotic series of repetitions in the first solo violin, which we show simply as a rhythmic entity:

You can identify the work by simply tapping out the rhythm and most musicians will recognize it. At the same time the second solo violin is establishing an equally powerful counter-rhythm:

A few bars later yet a third counter-rhythm is added:

This kind of intense rhythmic concentration is repeated not only throughout this work but throughout the opus as a whole. In the slow movement, Vivaldi grips our attention in another, equally compelling fashion. He first provides a grand dotted kind of French Overture, which leads to one of his magician-like sections, marked Larghetto, in which the violins each have a separate pattern which continues, bar after bar, page after page, in one of his characteristically compelling vignettes (see also Appendix III):

44

The opening of the slow movement in Opus 3, No. 10, Concerto for four violins.

Vivaldi's international publishing career had begun. It was soon to continue along equally sensational lines with Roger and his successors in Amsterdam, now becoming a centre of music publishing.

All this time, the printing of music was still an imperfect technique, and Italy was by no means in the forefront. Speaking of the poor quality of Italian editions of those days, Walter Kolneder writes[5]

> The Italians still assembled the staves from single printing stamps and each note with a tail had its own block, separated from the preceding and following ones. Such a procedure was possibly still good enough for older vocal music, but not so for groups of semiquavers and demisemiquavers in instrumental works. Roger was one of the first to join the shorter notes of a basic rhythmical value together with a single beam, and thus, simply by a graphic division of the sequence of notes, made it easier to get a quick idea of the music, facilitating sight-reading. His great commercial successes were not least dependent on these modern printing methods, and allowed him a wide range of activity as a publisher, especially of Italian orchestral and chamber music. Besides this he was the inventor of numbered publications for the convenience of listing and ordering works, for previously the numbers had only served to keep stored printing blocks in order.

What this means can be seen graphically if we reproduce a page from the Opus 2 violin sonatas: the bass line of the first gathering is particularly off-putting, as is the next (top) stave in the violin part. If we compare this to one of Estienne Roger's editions, we understand what Vivaldi meant when he wrote, in the introduction of his Estienne Roger edition of *L'estro armonico*, the following note 'for the dilettanti of music':

> The polite reception with which you have favoured my modest offerings has persuaded me to offer you an opus of instrumental concertos. I must, however, confess that in the past my compositions, partly from their defects, have been subjected in

addition to a poor standard of printing. Now they will have the major advantage of being engraved by the celebrated hand of Monsieur Estienne Roger. This was a reason for my having decided to satisfy you with the publication of the concertos and gives me the courage soon to present you with another set of concertos for four instruments. Keep me in your kind remembrance, and be happy.[6]

The set was dedicated to Ferdinand III of Tuscany, as follows:

Altezza Reale,
This opus may gain but little approval from your knowledgeable, formidable and truly sovereign judgement, but it is offered with all the devotion of a humble heart to the boundless merit of Your Royal Highness, although it bears no proportion to your venerable greatness. I myself had indeed subscribed to such an unfortunate opinion had I not upon reflection considered the misfortune from which it derives: The Prince, because he can not be recognised as he merits, must show indulgence from his height for those that just can be seen at his feet, and the people, because they can not make offerings as they should, must overcome with a great heart the misfortunes which their conditions bring.

Be it as it may, let this small tribute of my humblest devotion remain what it actually is; I know that you look not upon that what is offered but on the real humility of the one who offers it and I can have full confidence in the infinite graciousness of your elevated mind which spurns nothing and welcomes all. This truth also delivers me from the criticism that such reverence might be indiscreet. It grants me the exceptional courage to place myself humbly before your throne and to declare with this outward act of submission the respectful intention which alone drove me to invent the means whereby the public may have a vivid testimony that I consider myself always your most humble, devoted and obedient servant.

Antonio Vivaldi

For Opus 4 ('La Stravaganza'), Vivaldi provided a dedication to Vettor Delfino, a member of a celebrated Venetian noble family:

Excellency, it is the custom of everybody who dares to present the public with a work of his composition to recommend it to the authority of a great name, who should defend it against the garrulity of evil tongues and the heavily applied severity of the critics. I can not wish for a better protection of my feeble works than that of Your Excellency. Your great character which has distinguished itself in many fields is known also to the world of music. Your good taste in it has reached such a perfection that there is no artist who would not wish for the glory of having you as his master. I, who had the good fortune to be more your friend than your guide, never believed to have created something of quality had I not your approval. To you, therefore, more than to anybody else, is due this dedication of my efforts; so much the more that I have, for a long time, the honour to call myself Your Excellency's most humble, devoted and obedient servant,

Antonio Vivaldi

The problem of movable type recurred with second editions. After one edition had been sold out, and a new one was required, the type had to be reset all over again. With Estienne Roger's engraved plate, however, all that was required was to run off some more copies as needed. Hence Italian music publishing became more and more isolated. Gradually most of the important editions of Italian instrumental music were published in Amsterdam, later in Paris, which was about to become the music-publishing capital of the Continent. Operas were rarely published at all and thus could be even more rapidly forgotten; no doubt this accounts for at least some of the immediate neglect of Vivaldi's stage works. On the other hand, Italian instrumental music flourished as never before in the hands of the Dutch and French publishers. Soon the style became international and took root locally, with special success in Paris, Germany and Vienna – where at the time of Vivaldi's death there, a whole local school had grown up and was about to become, in the young Joseph Haydn's hands, the greatest instrumental school of music in the history of Europe up to that time. In the thematic catalogue of music owned by the Princes Esterházy in Eisenstadt we find, among many items of Italian music, *The Four Seasons* by Antonio Vivaldi. The connection is thus established.

IV
Violin Wizard

%

At the height of the Carnival season of 1715, there arrived at Venice another distinguished visitor from the North, Johann Friedrich Armand von Uffenbach, architect from Frankfurt-am-Main, who was a great amateur of music; he had presented *L'estro armonico* in 1713 to Strasbourg and marvelled at its reception; now, he had decided to travel to the lagoon city.[1]

He went to the Teatro San Angelo on 4 February 1715, when he writes in his diary:

I stayed here [at the casino] until it was time to leave for the opera, when I went with some acquaintances to the Teatro San Angelo, which is smaller and less dear than the one mentioned above [SS. Giovanni e Paolo]; its impresario was the celebrated Vivaldi, who also composed the opera, which was very charming and also most seductive to the eye; the theatre machinery is not as expensive as in the other theatres and the orchestra not so big, but nevertheless it was well worth attending. For fear of being badly treated and spat upon as in the large opera house [SS. Giovanni e Paolo, where someone had 'spit a disgusting gob' – *ein entsetzliches Maul* – on his libretto from the balcony] we took a box – it was not very expensive – and revenged ourselves in the local fashion [by spitting orange peels, etc.] on the parterre just as had been done to us the last time, which seemed to me to be quite impossible ... [but] the singers were excellent and not at all inferior to those of the big house, particularly some of the women, among them the so-called Fabri [Anna Maria Fabbri] was outstanding for her musicality as well as for her charm. She was, moreover, very beautiful; at least she looked so on the stage

49

... Towards the end Vivaldi played a solo accompaniment excellently, and at the conclusion he added a free fantasy [an improvised cadenza] which absolutely astounded me, for it is hardly possible that anyone has ever played, or ever will play, in such a fashion. He put his fingers but a hair's breadth from the bridge, so that there was scarcely room for the bow, and he did this on all four strings with fugues [*mit Fugen*, i.e. in imitation] and with incredible speed. Everyone was astounded, but it can hardly be described as captivating, for it was more deftly played than pleasing to the ear.

The distinguished German music historian Walter Kolneder has identified the concerto performed as probably that in D, RV212 (Pincherle, 165). (See Appendix V.)

It used to be thought that Pietro Locatelli (1695–1764), the brilliant Bergamasque violinist and composer, had enlarged the violin technique up to the fourteenth and fifteenth positions, codified in his Opus 3 (*XII Concerti cioè Violino solo con XXIV Capricci ad Libitum*), published in 1733 but obviously composed earlier and there 'gathered' in a single opus. It is now clear, however, that Vivaldi's role in the development of violin technique is as important historically as his eminence in the field of composition.

The opera that Uffenbach heard was probably L.A. Predieri's *Lucio Papiro*,[2] perhaps with additions by Vivaldi apart from his showy violin cadenzas in the interpolated violin concerto.

On 19 February Uffenbach went to hear the pasticcio *Nerone fatto Cesare* which he lists as *Agrippina* – see above, p. 35 – and liked neither the subject nor the mismatched costumes and, moreover, 'Vivaldi himself performed a solo on the violin only in a very small aria.' A few days later he heard the revised *Nerone* and liked it much better, attending two performances, on 28 February and 4 March,[3] and Vivaldi's stupendous performance on the violin so delighted him that Uffenbach decided to make the composer's acquaintance, which he duly recorded in his diary as follows:[4]

Wednesday 6 March 1715. After dinner Vivaldi, the famous composer and violinist, came to my home, for I sent invitations to him a number of times. I spoke of some concerti grossi that I would like to have from him, and I ordered them from him. For him, since he belonged to the Cantores [church musicians, who were reputed to be addicted to the bottle], some bottles of wine were ordered. He then let me hear some very difficult and quite inimitable improvisations [*Phantasien*] on the violin. From close by, I had to admire his skill all the more, and I saw quite clearly that he played unusual and lively pieces, to be sure, but in a way that lacked both charm and a *cantabile* manner.

Saturday 9 March 1715. In the afternoon Vivaldi came to me and brought me, as had been ordered, ten concerti grossi, which he said had been composed expressly for me. I bought some of them. In order that I might hear them better he wanted to teach me to play them at once, and on that account he would come to me from time to time. And thus we were to start this very day.

It was, of course, a *politesse* (not to put too fine a point on it) to tell Uffenbach that the ten concertos had been composed between 6 and 9 March: obviously Vivaldi raided his copious library, though, as Kendall reminds us,[5] we should not forget that the composer was quite capable, as in the case of *Tito Manlio*, of writing an entire opera in five days.

All this operatic activity did Vivaldi's reputation no good at the Pietà, where on 29 March 1716, the governors reversed their decision of 1715, when it had appeared (see above, p. 38) that they had come to terms with their *maestro di musica*'s double profession. Now they voted him only seven to five – a two-thirds majority was necessary – as *maestro di violino*, his advantage being reduced by a vote in a succeeding ballot. A few months later, Vivaldi had been hard at work and on 24 May he managed to have himself re-engaged as *Maestro de'Concerti* (was the different title significant?). To celebrate the event, he composed one of his most famous religious works, *Juditha triumphans*, the 'sacred military oratorio' which reminded Venetian audiences of their war with the Ottoman Empire and in particular their grim siege on the island of Corfu, of vital strategic importance to the Serenissima's presence in the Adriatic. Judith, of course, represents the Adriatic and hence Venice, and Holophernes the Sultan.

That summer of 1716 proved to be a vital one for the Republic. On 7 August 1716, the Holy Office of the Inquisition approved the text of *Juditha triumphans* and ten days later the Turkish commander, whose country had been disastrously defeated at Peterwardein by the almost legendary Prince Eugene of Austria on 5 August, decided to mount an all-out attack on Corfu, to be defeated again even more decisively.[6]

It was indeed an occasion to celebrate, and when the new oratorio was performed at the Pietà in November 1716, the whole panoply of the Ospedale's very considerable resources was put on display for the triumphant event – two *flûtes à bec* (recorders), two oboes, soprano chalumeau, two clarinets, two trumpets, timpani, four theorboes, mandolin, solo organ, four *viole all'inglese*, *viola d'amore*, and the full complement of strings. The presence of trumpets and kettledrums, the latter rare in Vivaldi's (and other Venetian) church music, recalls the war-like origins of the libretto.

This was not the first of Vivaldi's oratorios. Two years before, the Pietà had put on his *Moyses Deus Pharaonis*, of which only the libretto, with the *figlie* entered in handwriting, survives.[7]

There were no documented reactions to *Judith* at the Pietà in November 1716, but that year saw the arrival in Venice of a young German violin virtuoso in the service of the court at Dresden: Johann Georg Pisendel (1687–1755), an almost exact contemporary of J.S. Bach's. Pisendel, who arrived in Venice in April 1716, was one of a group of four chamber musicians sent to Italy to become part of the retinue of the Crown Prince Elector of Saxony, Frederick Augustus. Pisendel remained in Venice for the rest of 1716, returning there the next year. He collected a large quantity of Vivaldi's music, partly in the composer's autograph, which ended up in the Sächsische Landesbibliothek in Dresden and are known to Vivaldi scholarship as the 'Dresden Manuscripts'. They are a vital and authentic record of the composer at this exuberantly successful period of his creative life.

Pisendel's biography, as recounted in instalments in Johann Adam Hiller's *Wöchentliche Nachrichten und Anmerkungen, die Musik betreffend*,[8] has the following interesting anecdotes about his life in Venice:

... During his [Pisendel's] stay in Venice, two curious and very different occurrences happened. The first is as follows: once he was required by the Saxon Crown Prince Elector to play a violin concerto in the orchestra between the acts of an opera (I don't know if at S. Gristosomo [*sic*] or S. Angelo) – presumably because ballets were not then as customary in the operas as they are today. He chose one in F with hunting horns by Vivaldi which begins as follows [theme = RV 571]. The last movement of this concerto begins as follows [theme]. In this last movement the solo part begins with a *cantabile*. At the end there is, however, a long passage with demisemiquavers which lie in the highest positions ... During this passage the gentlemen of the orchestra, who were all Italians, speeded up the accompaniments in order to discomfort Herr Pisendel. But he paid no attention to their increased speed, which was supposed to dig his grave, and by stamping his feet in time loudly he put them all to shame. The Prince was particularly pleased about that ... The second curious occurrence which befell Herr Pisendel in Venice was as follows:

He was walking with Herr Vivaldi on St. Mark's Square. In the middle of the walk Vivaldi took him aside and said he must come home with him [Vivaldi] at once. Herr Pisendel did so right away and Vivaldi told him en route that four policemen, unbeknown to Herr Pisendel, were following him continually and keeping him under exact observation. He asked Herr Pisendel earnestly if he had perhaps done something illegal in Venice, and when Herr Pisendel could recall having done nothing of the sort, [Vivaldi] advised him not to leave the house until he, Herr Vivaldi, could investigate the situation and let him know what was happening. Herr Vivaldi, who knew many people in Venice, went to speak forthwith to one of the State Inquisitors, and offered to vouch for Herr Pisendel's good character. But the Inquisitor answered that they were looking for a certain other person, whose dwelling they had meanwhile located. But because this other person looked like Herr Pisendel, the police had begun to follow him closely. Meanwhile Herr Pisendel could go where he wished, without any fears ...

For all its gay life, one should never forget that Venice was a police state – benevolent, in a certain sense perhaps, but the eye of the Serenissima was always fixed on strangers.

Meanwhile Vivaldi's position at the Pietà must have been less than satisfactory, and he is no longer listed on the Ospedale's paylists for 1717, nor did he attempt to be re-appointed in 1718. And from 1718 to 1722, Vivaldi's name disappears entirely from the records of the Pietà's governors. He was producing operas in Venice with some regularity – two in the year 1718 – but he had meanwhile found a brilliant new position in the nearby town of Mantua.

❉   ❉   ❉

Famous among music-lovers because of its largely infamous role in Claudio Monteverdi's life, the former duchy of the Gonzaga family had fallen on evil times. It had become a pawn in the War of the Spanish Succession and had been invaded and brutally sacked by the Imperial troops in the previous century. The Austrians had made of Mantua a hereditary fief and had appointed a governor in the person of the younger brother, Prince Philipp, of the Landgrave of Hesse-Darmstadt. Our knowledge of Vivaldi's stay in Mantua comes from the best evidence, an autograph letter of 16 November 1737 to Marchese Guido Bentivoglio d'Aragona, wherein the composer writes, 'In Mantova sono stato tre anni al servigio dell piissimo principe Darmstadt' ('In Mantua I was for three years in the service of the late lamented Prince of Darmstadt'). The list of operas produced at Mantua – see Appendix I – shows that those three years were 1718–20.

As *Maestro di cappella da camera* at the Mantuan court, Vivaldi's duties seem to have extended only to secular music, which also included cantatas written for some special Mantuan occasions. The Austrian connection manifested itself in another unexpected way: Mantua, as an extension of the Austrian monarchy, featured one of the specialities imported from another part of the kingdom, and specifically Bohemia – hunting horn players. Michael Talbot reminds us that horns now begin to occupy a far more important role in Vivaldi's *oeuvre* than hitherto.[9] Thus it can be seen once again how eighteenth-century composers remained pragmatists, willingly subject to the exigencies of the court, or institution, to which they had attached themselves.

Some years ago, several new documents concerning Vivaldi's stay in Mantua came to light.[10] In the years between the spring of 1718 and the beginning of March 1720, Vivaldi's operatic activity in Mantua flourished, culminating in the Carnival season of 1719, wherein was celebrated the marriage between Philipp of Hesse-Darmstadt, the governor and Imperial Plenipotentiary of Mantua, and Eleonora of Guastalla. Two Vivaldi operas, *Teuzzone* and *Tito Manlio* were produced, after which the composer left for Florence, where the Teatro della Pergola was to be reopened with his opera *Scanderbeg*. Before leaving Vivaldi requested Carlo Bertazzoni, superintendant of the Archducal Treasury (*sovrintendente della Scalcheria Arciducale*), to allow free entrance to the theatre for certain members of the chancery as a token of appreciation for sundry favours received from them. A ticket cost sixty lire. The impresario of the theatre was Giovan Battista Carboni, a respected singer who was a member of the Archducal *Cappella* at Mantua, and he flatly refused this proposal. Perhaps this refusal was connected with the composer having decamped for Florence. In 1720, Vivaldi's contribution to the Mantuan theatre was limited to composing one opera, *La Candace*, and among the documents in the Mantuan archives are two which show us the huge expenses involved in mounting operas for one Carnival season. A receipt signed by Vivaldi shows that he was earning 10 *Luigi* (*louis d'or*) per month, which was 680 lire, a very substantial sum of money (note that Vivaldi was paid for five months: the paragraph also explains the rate between *louis d'or* and lire).[11]

Danaro ricevuto, e pagato p[er] gli Virtuosi delle Opere del Carnovale pross.ᵐᵒ passato.

Loggie fin questo giorno 28 Febr.o 1720.	£.	4917
Biribis	»	1140
Per Scene	»	2000
Da S.A.S.	»	7100,10
	£.	15157,10

Danaro pagato alli Virtuosi sodetti, come Siegue.

Sig.ᵃ Guglielmini	£.	1872
Sig.ᵃ Zoboli	»	1333,18
S.ᵉ Barbieri	»	1420
S.ᵉ Speroncini	»	1890
S.ᵉ Cortoncino	»	7000

Sig.ᵉ D. Antonio Vivaldi reliquato delle Loggie,
a conto de suoi sallarij di mesate cinque, in
raggione di Luigi dieci al mese da £. 68 L'una,

come dall'Ordine	»	1576,12
	£.	15092,10

Al Coñesso, p[er] la riscossa del danaro de

Palchetti secondo il Solito	»	65
	£.	15157,10

Fatte pagare da S.A.S. alla S.ᵃ Zani, col mezzo del S.ʳ David Sinitta
£. 4900

Adi 26 febr o. 1720
O' ricevute io sotto scritto dal Sig.ʳ Carlo Bertazzon Sovra-
intendente della Scalcheria Arcid:ˡᵉ lire mille cinquecento-
Settantasei, e soldi dodici, e queste a conto delle lire tremila e
quattro cento, che sono Luigi cinquanta da lire sessant'otto l'una
da pagarmi secondo l'ordine preciso di S.A.S. il Sig.ʳ Prē.pe
Governatore Padrone, dico … £. 1576,12

D. An:º Vivaldi aff:º

The termination of Vivaldi's operatic activities in Mantua was a
result of the death on 19 January 1720 of the Empress in Vienna,
Eleonore Magdalena Theresa, widow of Leopold I, as a conse-
quence of which all theatres in the monarchy were closed. Vivaldi at
once procured a letter of recommendation to the Imperial Ambassador in Venice, Count Colloredo.[12]

In 1723 Vivaldi's official position at the Pietà was renewed, with a
Notatorio on 2 July, wherein it is stipulated that the composer (who
had just delivered two concertos for the Visitation of the Blessed
Virgin Mary) was to provide two more concertos every month, even
when he was absent from Venice; the postage was to be charged to

the Pietà. He was to direct three or four rehearsals for each concert when he was in Venice to see that the young ladies are 'in good condition to play properly'. The composer appears in the records of the governors until 1725, when a huge gap – a decade, no less – begins. Vivaldi's presence was becoming scarce in Venice.

In the autumn of the year before Vivaldi's name disappears so dramatically from the Pietà's pay-lists, a young singer from Mantua ('mantovana') made her first appearance in the Teatro S. Moisè in Venice, as Clistere in Albinoni's *Laodice*. (She is also reported to have been born in Venice as the daughter of a French wig-maker, the truth of which her Italianized name, Giraud = Girò, would seem to confirm.) In any case she was to become a scintillating contralto singer and Vivaldi's pupil; the description 'mantovana' may simply mean that she acquired her reputation in that town. Since her life, together with that of her sister, was about to be linked with Vivaldi's for the next fourteen years, we shall make a pause in our narrative of the composer's life and return to Amsterdam, where ten days before Christmas Eve in 1725 the *Gazette d'Amsterdam* announced Vivaldi's Opus VIII, *Il cimento dell'armonia e dell'inventione*, the 'Contest between harmony and invention', or between the 'science of composition' (as Haydn used to call it) and inspiration. Le Cène's new edition was again a gathering of works already known in manuscript copies, as Vivaldi candidly admitted in his introductory dedication to Count Morzin (a relative of Haydn's patron of the 1750s in Lukavec in Bohemia); he makes special reference in this regard to the first four concertos, *Le quattro stagioni* (*The Four Seasons*). Neither Le Cène nor Vivaldi could possibly have imagined that two centuries later it would become the most popular piece of classical music in the world; and it is to this extraordinary work that we must now turn our attention.

V

'The Four Seasons'

❧

*T*he *Four Seasons* has become so famous – it is regularly used for television advertising, as background music in restaurants, as film music – that many people never realize that Vivaldi was writing programme music. In fact, the score closely follows the sonnets (written by himself?) with which the score is prefaced in the first edition by Charles le Cène. Not only does Vivaldi print the sonnets *in extenso* but provides them with large letters ('A', 'B', etc.) in the left margins referring to the places in the music which illustrate any given text.

Since, for many people, these sonnets will be new, we print them here, first in the amusing Italian, or rather Venetian, found in Le Cène's elegant edition, followed by a prose translation (the author's).

PRIMAVERA

Giunt' è la Primavera e festosetti
   La salutan gl' Augei con lieto canto,
E i fonti allo spirar de Zeffiretti
   Con dolce mormorio scorrono intanto:

   Vengon' coprendo l'aer di nero amanto
E Lampi, e tuoni ad annuntiarla eletti
Indi tacendo questi, gl'Augelletti,
   Tornan' di nuovo al lor canoro incanto:

E quindi sul fiorito ameno prato
   Al caro mormorio di fronde e piante
Dorme'l Caprar col fido can' à lato.

Di pastoral Zampogna al suon festante
Danzan Ninfe e Pastor nel tetto amato
Di primavera all'apparir brillante.

SPRING

Spring has come and with it gaiety,
The birds salute it with joyous song,
And the brooks, caressed by Zephyr's breath,
Flow meanwhile with sweet murmurings:

The sky is covered with dark clouds,
Announced by lightning and thunder.
But when they are silenced, the little birds
Return to fill the air with their song:

Then does the meadow, in full flower,
Ripple with its leafy plants.
The goat-herd dozes, guarded by his faithful dog.

Rejoicing in the pastoral bagpipes,
Nymphs and Shepherds dance, in love,
Their faces glowing with Springtime's brilliance.

All four concertos, one to each season, must have provided cameo roles for Vivaldi, for all are scored for 'Violino principale', two violins (*ripieno*), violas, violoncellos and double basses with continuo. In Gian Francesco Malipiero's historic first edition in score of 1950, the continuo was assigned to organ 'or harpsichord', but nowadays the latter is usually preferred. (Malipiero suggested using both and that was the way in which the first Cetra recording was issued.) In my brief analysis, we also draw attention to supplementary descriptive titles not in the prefatory sonnets, such as the incredible indication of a dog barking in this first concerto.

The bright E major opening of 'La Primavera' has won friends all over the world, ever since its first publication by Le Cène. Although it is not the purpose of this book to enter into complicated musical analyses, we must point out that the 'binding' motive of this first allegro is the clever alteration of quavers with a pair of semiquavers, which lends to the music a forward impulse very characteristic of its composer, as are the echoing fortes and pianos. In the middle of bar fourteen the solo violin and the (solo) leader of the first violins imitate the bird calls (*Canto dè gl'uccelli*), with short and longer trills and repeated quavers – all utterly delightful. A little later, after a shortened entry of the main subject, we plunge into a lifelike description of streams ruffled by breezes (running violins in softly undulating semiquavers, *piano*, which effortlessly transfer themselves to the basses before we are given the leitmotiv again. This time we plunge into a storm, with thunder and lightning – the repeated demisemiquavers alternating with scales rushing upwards, and then the solo violin in triplets imitating lightning: this was surely the basis for Haydn's famous triplet figures in the flutes when, in his *The Seasons*, he introduces his great storm in Part II (Summer), No. 17 of 1801. After the storm we return yet again to the opening leitmotiv, to introduce the birds returning to their songs.

The next movement sets the scene for the third strophe of the sonnet. The solo violin, in dreamy melody, represents the sleeping goat-herd. The two violins move in quiet dotted rhythms, telling us of the meadows rippling under a soft May wind. In an incredible stroke of genius, the entire rest of the music is given to the violas, 'sempre *f* si deve suonare sempre molto forte e stroppato' (always *f*, to be played very loudly throughout and raspingly), which describe 'il cane che grida', the dog which many of us have heard, howling or barking at the moon on a still moonlit night in a solitary northern Italian landscape. Vivaldi has even caught the dog's rhythm – woof-*woof*, woof-*woof*, woof-*woof*. It is an eerie moment and, in my opinion, it reveals a private side of its composer's personality in a rare disclosure. This is genuinely lonely music, of a profound beauty but also with a deep sense of sadness. This is not the dramatic tragedy of northern European scores but quiet, unsentimental music which immediately touches the heart. Characteristically, the whole movement is given to this one scene.

The rustic dance which follows is in the bagpipes rhythm of 12/8, with the violins muted to make the description more realistic. Again, the entire Allegro describes only the last three lines of the sonnet. It is in three parts, with the main idea placed in the minor for the middle section. Music historians have noted that Vivaldi requires a new notation to accent the end of a phrase in the solo violin, a little figure that is repeated endlessly:

L'ESTADE (ESTATE)

Sotto dura staggion dal sole accesa
    Langue l'huom, langue 'l gregge, ed arde il Pino,°
Scioglie, il cucco la Voce, e tosto intesa
    Canta la Tortorella e'l gardelino.†

Zeffiro dolce spira, mà contesa
    Muove Borea improviso al suo vicino,
E piange il Pastorel, perche sospesa
    Teme fiera borasca, e'l suo destino,

Toglie alle membra lasse il suo riposo
    Il timore de' Lampi, e tuoni fieri
E de mosche, e mossoni il stuol furioso!

    Ah che pur troppo i suoi timor son veri
Tuona e fulmina il Ciel e grandinoso
    Tronca il capo alle spiche e a'grani alteri°°

° Piano [?] suggestion by Gian Francesco Malipiero, 1950
† 'Gardelino', Venetian for 'cardellino'.
°° Giazotto, 1965, suggests 'a' grand' alberi'

SUMMER

Under the heavy season of a burning sun,
Man languishes, his herd wilts, the pine° is parched
The cuckoo finds its voice, and chiming in with it
The turtle-dove, the goldfinch.

Zephyr breathes gently but, contested,
The North-wind appears nearby and suddenly:
The shepherd sobs because, uncertain,
He fears the wild squall and its effects:

His weary limbs have no repose, goaded by
His fear of lightning and wild thunder;
While gnats and flies in furious swarms surround him.

Alas, his fears prove all too grounded,
Thunder and lightning split the Heavens, and hail-stones
Slice the top of the corn and other grain.‡

° Or, following Malipiero, 'the plain is
parched'.
‡ Or, following Giazotto, 'great trees'.

'L'Estade' has a bold beginning, describing the stifling heat of an August noon: we are in G minor, and the off-beat quavers seem to have difficulty in breathing – how like one of those leaden days in the Veneto, when the white dust of the roads suffocates man and beast. In a sudden switch of mood, the solo violin is given a long section of virtuoso brilliance: underneath, the cuckoo sings a curiously abrupt dotted figure in the bass line, to be swallowed up by the whole string orchestra taking over the virtuoso part of the solo violin. After a brief return to the breathless beginning – how clear Vivaldi is in his formal patterns! – we are told that the turtle-dove is singing, to be followed by the goldfinch. The turtle-dove has some very odd dissonances between solo violin (*A flat*) and the empty, i.e. continuo-less, base line (*G*). The goldfinch has trills and very high alternating notes, which merge seamlessly into triplets, for the upper strings, telling us of soft summer winds (bars 78ff.). Suddenly (bar 90) the north wind sweeps into the proceedings, and the full orchestra gives us another dramatic storm, with dashing violinistic figures on the top. Again the breathless opening, this time leading us to the frightened peasant, against whom the north wind blows angrily.

The next Adagio alternates between gnats and flies (dotted repeated notes under the languid solo violin) and angry thunder (whole orchestra). The peasant's fears are justified, and the north-wind returns in an enormous movement (Presto) which concludes the concerto. There are more brilliant sections for the solo violin, and this G minor outburst concludes 'Summer' – a striking contrast to the contented pages, even with interruptions, of 'Spring'.

L'AUTUNNO

Celebra il Vilanel con balli e Canti
    Del felice raccolto il bel piacere
E del liquor di Bacco accesi tanti
    Finiscono col sonno il lor godere

Fa ch'ogn' uno tralasci e balli e canti
    L'aria che temperata dà piacere,
E la staggion ch' invita tanti e tanti
    D'un dolcissimo sonno al bel godere.

I cacciator alla nov' alba à caccia
    Con corni, schioppi, e canni escono fuore
Fugge la belua, e seguono la traccia,

    Già sbiogottita, e lassa al gran rumore
De' schioppi e canni ferita minaccia
    Languida di fuggir, mà oppressa muore.

AUTUMN

The country-folk celebrate, with dance and song,
The joy of gathering a bountiful harvest.
With Bacchus's liquor, quaffed liberally,
Their joy finishes in slumber.

Each one renounces dance and song
The mild air is pleasant
And the season invites ever increasingly
To savour a sweet slumber.

The hunters at dawn go to the hunt,
With horns and guns and dogs they sally forth,
The beasts flee, their trail is followed:

Already dismay'd and exhausted, from the great noise
Of guns and dogs, threaten'd with wounds,
They flee, languishing, and die, cowering.

Autumn is in F major and begins with 'dances and songs' of the country-folk, content with their harvest: another set-piece of great rhythmic force, repeated in thirds by the solo violin. All this literally disintegrates into drunken semiquaver arpeggios and falling octaves, between which the first five notes of the main theme try, without much success, to establish themselves. At bars 41ff. the violin solo is falling about ('drunks', 'ubriachi', notes Le Cène's edition). The drunks trill up the scale, then hiccup in syncopations (bars 54ff.). The un-drunk farmers continue their dancing with the opening leitmotiv but a drunk (bars 67ff.) disturbs the proceedings, reeling up and down in the solo violin – how Vivaldi must have relished playing this part – and finally winding up in a curiously moving section describing 'L'ubriaco che dorme', 'the drunk asleep' (bars 89ff.), where everything slows down, the solo violin in long notes, the other violins in repeated quavers, to which the viola adds a long series of slow-moving notes by way of a bass part (bars 97ff.). The un-drunk peasants win out and conclude this delightful movement.

Adagio molto is the title of the next movement, describing the drunks sound asleep. It is one of the most extraordinary sections of the whole cycle, all the strings muted and stealing in among us like so many thieves. Malipiero provided a famous and brilliantly original harpsichord part with the right hand threading a long, golden line in quavers among the sleeping strings. It may or may not be the kind of continuo that Vivaldi expected or even wanted, but it is very beautiful and once heard is not easily discarded. Vivaldi instructed the harpsichord: 'Il cembalo arpeggia'.

La caccia, or the hunt, is the next movement, and this Allegro tells us why the whole of 'Autumn' was placed in F major: because it is the key of the hunting horn (not, to be sure, the only key but the one which would have been most easily recognised as the key of *la chasse*, e.g. Bach's Brandenburg Concerto No. 1 with its solo horns or the F major part of Handel's *Water Music*, with its introduction of horns to musical London). And as soon as the solo violin arrives on the scene (bar 190) we find it in thirds, fourths and fifths, imitating the notes a French horn could play at the time (i.e. the notes of the harmonic scale). Later, after a series of dazzling sextuplets (bars 219ff.) in the solo violin, we are taken back to the main theme. This is always Vivaldi's method of keeping the movement together formally, and it is unfailingly efficient and successful: it keeps our feet on the ground, so to say, after the extravagant fantasies that have gone before. The animals seek to escape (triplets in the solo violin, bars 236ff.), guns are fired at them, the dogs bay with excitement (wild repeated thirds). The leitmotiv appears again in between the hysterical manœuverings of the fleeing beasts, but exhausted, they die (dogs' bayings accompany their dying gasps). But Vivaldi's, and the *settecento*'s, sense of order prevails; and the opening dotted passage once again intervenes, and, with it, this amazingly original and inventive third concerto concludes.

L'INVERNO

Aggiacciato tremar tra nevi algenti
   Al severo spirar d'orrido Vento,
   Correr battendo i piedi ogni momento,
E pel soverchio gel batter i denti

Passar al foco i di quieti e contenti
   Mentre la pioggio [*sic*]fuor bagna ben cento
   Caminar sopra 'l giaccio, e a passo lento
Per timor di cader gersene intenti,

Gir forte sdruzziolar, cader a terra
   Di nuovo ir sopra 'l giaccio e correr forte
Sin ch'il giaccio si rompe, e si disserra,

   Sentir uscir dalle ferrate porte
Sirocco Borea, e tutti i Venti in guerra
   Quest' e verno, ma tal, che gioja apporte.

WINTER

Frozen and trembling among the chilly snow,
Our breathing hampered by horrid winds,
As we run, we stamp our feet continuously,
Our teeth chatter with the frightful cold:

We move to the fire and contented peace,
While the rain outside pours in sheets.

Now we walk on the ice, with slow steps,
Attentive how we walk, for fear of falling;

If we move quickly, we slip and fall to earth,
Again walking heavily on the ice,
Until the ice breaks and dissolves;

We hear from the closed doors
Boreas and all the winds at war –
This is winter, but such as brings joy.

'L'Inverno', or 'Winter', is in F minor, which is also the key of several 'Sleighride' pieces for orchestra by Leopold Mozart and Franz Georg Wassmuth, when a woman trembling with the winter cold is described ('8. Hört man ein *Adagio* welches das vor Kälte zitternde Frauenzimmer vorstellet' / '8th is an *Adagio* in which is described a woman trembling with cold'). Here, Vivaldi's string orchestra enters, a part at a time, beginning with the bass, to tell us of a frozen landscape in the Veneto, the humans 'frozen and trembling' (the latter = trills in the violins). 'Horrid winds' enter, represented by the solo violin. Later, in a fierce section (bars 22ff.) our legs are shaking with the cold; and at bars 47ff., there are double stops in the solo violin to imitate chattering teeth.

The second movement, a Largo, describes sitting in front of the fire while the rain (violins pizzicato) beats outside, all in a contented E flat. Anyone who has experienced a driving rain in the Veneto will remember the delight of escaping into a room with a roaring open fire, spits of game turning slowly in front of it.

In the next movement, Allegro, the basses are instructed (in Malipiero's edition) to use long bowings, while the violin solo slithers about in quavers with no supporting harmonies whatever: this is walking on thin ice, and after two pages of score we slide carefully into slurred quavers – walking very carefully so as not to slip. But we try just the same to walk quickly and do slip, falling (solo violin, bars 121ff.); we try again, with staccato semiquavers. At bar 170 the ice breaks. The south wind blows outside the tightly fastened doors in another beautiful Lento which, with hesitant pauses, leads to a violent series of passages in the solo violin (bars 201ff.): the north wind arrives and gives battle to all the other winds.

And with this dazzling exhibition of Vivaldi's skill as a violinist matched with his audacity as a composer, we hurtle to the conclusion, not really encouraged by Vivaldi's comforting words that this is a winter 'such as brings joy'. But *The Four Seasons* has certainly brought joy to what is now quite literally millions of people all over the civilized world – a situation which would certainly have astonished Vivaldi, who considered himself in many ways to be a modest cog in the universe.

The original edition was dedicated to Count Venceslas von Morzin, of a noble Bohemian family, one member of which would be Haydn's patron in the 1750's.

Most illustrious Sir,
while thinking of the many years in which I have had the great good fortune to serve your Illustrious Grace as Maestro di Musica in Italy, I was embarrassed when I considered that until now I have not given you any proof of the profound veneration I have for you; therefore I have decided to engrave the present volume and to submit it to the feet of Your Illustrious Grace; I beg you not to be surprised if among these few and feeble concertos, Your Illustrious Grace will find the Four Seasons, already long since under the indulgent and generous eye of Your Grace, but may you believe me that I took great pride in publishing them, because they are in any case the same, but enlarged, apart from the Sonnets, with a detailed explanation of everything in them and I am sure they will seem new to you.

Therefore I continue to ask that Your Illustrious Grace look with benevolence and indulgence on my feeble efforts, because I fear to offend the inborn kindness which Your Illustrious Grace has shown towards them for some time.

The great understanding for music possessed by Your Illustrious Grace and the high standard of your brilliant virtuoso orchestra allow me to rest assured that my poor efforts – now in your esteemed hands – will find the echo they merit. Otherwise it remains for me to implore your Grace to continue your most generous patronage of one who has the honour to subscribe himself, Your Grace's most humble, devoted and obedient servant, Antonio Vivaldi

The earlier version of *The Four Seasons* to which Vivaldi refers in this dedication has in fact come down to us in a collection of manuscript music formerly owned by Cardinal Pietro Ottoboni in Rome and sold after his death. This collection, which is very substantial, found its way to England and is now in the Henry Watson Library in Manchester. They have been published in facsimile by the Garland Press in New York (1991) and have been examined in a series of three articles by Paul Everett.[1]

Christopher Hogwood has scored up the Ottoboni Version of *The Four Seasons* and has it in the repertory of his orchestra, the Academy of Ancient Music.

VI
Venice, Mantua and Rome

❦

In the Autumn of 1720 Vivaldi returned from Mantua to the Teatro San Angelo in Venice to produce a new opera, *La verità in cimento*. The maestro seems to have been responsible for casting his new opera, 'because' as Eleanor Selfridge-Field[1] points out, 'the principal roles were all taken by singers in the employ of persons who were important past or future patrons of his.' The first performance was on 27 October 1720. In that very month the authorities permitted Vivaldi's aristocratic colleague Benedetto Marcello to publish a satire, soon to become famous, entitled 'Il Teatro alla moda'. On the title page of this treatise is an engraving of a rowing boat with three figures in it. One is a bear, in the bow, harbouring a keg of wine and other provisions; this refers to Giovanni Orsato (Orsati, Orsatti: 'orso' in Italian = bear), impresario of the Teatro S. Moisè. The other large figure with the oars is obviously the impresario of San Angelo, Modotto, who had been in the boat trade, an eminently suitable occupation for a man in Venice. But the most amusing figure in this engraving is the little angel at the helm with a priestly hat, playing the violin, one foot on the rudder and the other raised as if in a dancing position, or gesticulating – the 'red priest' in his role as music master at San Angelo theatre and in the impressum referred to as 'Aldivi'. Vivaldi comes in for many barbs in the book: accompaniments with upper strings only, or with the whole orchestra in unison, or with solos for exotic instruments. It used to be thought, in the words of Michael Talbot,[2] that 'throughout the book Vivaldi is obviously a prime target.' And, as Remo Giazotto has also observed, 'San Angelo was their [the Marcello family's] property'.[3]

Titlepage of Marcello's satire 'Il Teatro alla Moda'.

Nevertheless, Eleanor Selfridge-Field has aptly pointed out that the 'iconography of the title page of *Il teatro*, when discussed in the context of Vivaldi studies, always seems to bear heavily on Vivaldi, but partly because the current interest in all the other figures satirized is very little.' The title page reads as follows:

IL
TEATRO
ALLA MODA
OSIA

70

METODO sicuro, e facile per ben comporre, ed esequire
L'OPERE Italiane in Musica all'uso moderno.
Nel quale
Si danno Avvertimenti utili, e necessarja Poeti, Compo-
sitori di Musica, Musici dell'uno, e dell'altro sesso,
Impressarj, Suonatori, Ingegneri, e Pittori di Sce-
ne, Parti buffe, Sarti, Paggi, Comparse, Suggeri-
tori, Copisti, Protettori, e Madri di Virtuose, ed
altre Persone appartenenti al Teatro.
DEDICATO
DALL' AUTORE DEL LIBRO
AL COMPOSITORE DI ESSO.
Stampato ne'BORGHI di BELISANIA per ALDIVI.
VALICANTE; all'insegna dell'Orso in PEATA.
Si vende nella STRADA del CORALLO alla
PORTA del Palazzo d' ORLANDO.
E si ristamperà ogn'anno con nuova aggiunta.

The Theatre *à la mode*, or a sure and easy method for composing
Italian operas well, and fashioning them in a modern manner. In
which is contained useful and necessary instructions for poets,
musical composers, singers of both sexes, impresarios, players, stage
designers, scenery painters, *buffa* singers, tailors, pages, supers,
prompters, copyists, patrons and mothers of lady virtuosi, and other
persons belonging to the theatre. Dedicated by the author of the
book to its composer. Printed by Aldivi Valicante; in the Borghi di
Belisania at the Sign of the Bear in the Barque. To be had in the
Strada del Corallo at the Gate of the Palazzo d'Orlando. The book
will be reprinted annually with supplements.

Obviously 'Peata' has the double meaning of barque and 'Pietà'.
'Porta' refers to the composer Giovanni Porta and 'Orlando' to the
composer Giuseppe Maria Orlandini. 'Palazzo' = Giovanni Palazzi,
the librettist of Vivaldi's new opera, *La verità in cimento*. All these
names are as prominent as Vivaldi's. Other names and their
Marcello-anagrams are singers in the new opera: Chiara Orlandi
(= 'Orlando'), Anna Maria Strada ('Strada') and Antonia Laurenti
(= 'Corallo'). Since Bolognese singers had been appearing in Venice

71

with increasing frequency, we may surmise that two such imports, Domenico Borgi and Cecilia Belisania (or 'Ballisani') – the former served at the Mantuan court – are included in the imprimatur: they had sung at San Angelo during the season of autumn 1719. 'Licante' = Caterina Canteli, who was another Bolognese singer.

And now we come to the criticism of '*ariette* accompanied by *pizzicato* instruments, *trombe marine, piomè* [Jews' harp] ...'. Everyone has supposed that Marcello was lampooning Vivaldi's extravagantly orchestrated concertos, such as the 'Concerto con Due Flauti, Due Teorbi, Due Mandolini, Due Salmò, Due Violini in Tromba marina et un Violoncello' (RV 532), even though this is a work performed at the Pietà twenty years later in 1740: obviously it was not entirely isolated.

As it happens, the Marcello family were in litigation after 1718. According to Eleanor Selfridge-Field, Benedetto Marcello and the third brother Girolamo 'were favoured by their Uncle Nicolò, who was the last surviving brother of the parent generation, but Alessandro, the first-born of Agostino (father of Benedetto and Girolamo), seems none the less to have been significantly better off in terms of worldly possessions'.[4]

Why could not the gibe at exotic instruments be levelled at the concertos of Alessandro Marcello?, asks Eleanor Selfridge-Field. The brothers all belonged to a distinguished noble family, and it was regarded as distinctly *infra dig* for members of such a clan to be even semi-professional composers. Literary activity, on the other hand, was tolerantly accepted as a gentlemanly occupation, and we should perhaps regard the *Teatro* as that. Alessandro was educated in the art of writing sonnets, and their mother, Paolina Cappello, was a literary figure of some distinction, although her poetic works were destroyed by fire in 1745. Moreover, Benedetto Marcello's links with the Pietà were also close: his counterpoint teacher was Francesco Gasparini, who began to work for the institution in 1701, and to compose operas for the Teatro San Angelo in 1702 (*Tiberio, Imperatore d'oriente*).

As for Benedetto Marcello's objections to the ridiculously servile dedicatory prefaces in use at that time, it applies to many others as well as to Vivaldi. Vivaldi's prefaces have been quoted extensively in this book. Marcello advises that a composer should select as his dedicatee someone wealthy rather than cultured; the words 'Liberty', 'generous soul' (*animo generoso*), etc., must appear; and to conclude, the composer should kiss the flea bites on the legs of his Excellency's dog. Vivaldi in Opus 2's dedication kisses 'even the lowest steps of your throne', but many other composers' dedications are equally loathsome, as indeed are the cantata texts happily set to music during most of the eighteenth century.

And now we come to a new development in the relationship between Vivaldi and the Marcello family. The satire seems to have done Vivaldi no good. The *Teatro* was published in December 1720. For the carnival season for 1721, Vivaldi opened with *Filippo, rè di Macedonia* at San Angelo, but he composed only the last act (the rest was by Giuseppe Boniventi). After this production, Vivaldi wrote no more operas for Venice until 1725–6.[5]

At Mantua, too, he was no longer in active service as *maestro di cappella*, nor did Governor Philipp, brother of the Landgrave of Hesse-Darmstadt, replace him; perhaps this was simply an economic move. Perhaps the composer may have surmised that it was time to travel. What is most significant is the sudden change in repertoire at the Teatro San Angelo. Reinhard Strohm writes:[6]

> ... we now discover that the policy of S. Angelo changed with the beginning of carnival, 1721. Although the singers, on contract for the whole season, were staying ... the three carnival operas were strikingly different from *La verità in cimento*; the pastoral *Il pastor fido*, with a new libretto by Benedetto Pasqualigo from the 'maestro di coro' at the Pietà, Carlo Pietragrua; the heroic *Filippo, rè di Macedonia*, newly written [by the librettist Domenico] Lalli in which Vivaldi had only one act; and – probably last in the season – a revival of Pasqualigo's and Orlandini's *Antigona*, taken over from San Giovanni Grisostomo. The aesthetic change is a drastic one, also considering the outmoded style of Pietragrua's *Pastor fido*, the score of which is preserved. I feel it is unlikely that Vivaldi himself would have suggested works by Lalli, Pasqualigo, and particularly Orlandini, his biggest rival; it is far more likely that he lost control of the theatre. He ceased to write operas for Venice for more than four years – the longest interruption of this kind in his career. We

73

cannot help ascribing this, at least partly, to the effect of Marcello's satire.

Vivaldi's first attempt to secure a new position was in Milan. Here, his new work was a birthday tribute for the Empress Elisabeth, a 'drama pastorale' entitled *La Silvia*, performed at the Teatro Regio Ducale on 28 August 1721. There is no record of the public's (or Elisabeth's) reaction, but the fact that *La Silvia* led to no other operatic commission for Milan suggests that the reception was lukewarm. On the other hand, it cannot have been totally negative, for the Milan opera seems to have been ultimately responsible for another kind of work for the Lombard capital: the oratorio *L'adorazione delli tre rè magi*, produced there in 1722, the following year. The libretto survives, but the music is lost.

A further excursion away from Venetian theatre and Marcello proved to be the commission for a grand *Serenata* or Serenade in honour of the Princess of Sulzbach, who was married to the Prince of Piedmont at Vercelli on 15 March 1722, after which the company left for Turin. The *Mercure de France* for April 1722 tells us that[7]

La Princesse de Sultzback [*sic*] ... est arrivée à Brescia le même jour [11 mars] ... M. le Marquis Pietro Martinengo donna à souper à cette Princesse le soir du jour de son arrivée, & la regela ensuite d'une belle serenade.

An Italian report specifically identifies the composer – 'Cenato in pubblico in casa del marchese Pietro Martinengo fu udita una bellissima serenata e due concerti coi violini e gli oboé opera del monsignor A. Vivaldi' ('Dined in public at the house of Marchese Pietro Martinengo where they played a most beautiful serenade and two concertos with violins and oboes by Monsignor A. Vivaldi').[8] We cannot identify this Serenade, probably similar to one given fourteen years earlier at Rovigo in July 1708 to honour the departing Podestà and Captain, Francesco Querini. The music of Vivaldi's Serenade (RV 688), 'Le gare del dovere', is also lost, but at least we possess the complete printed libretto, with Vivaldi's dedication to Elena Minotti Querini, the Podestà's wife (copy in Milan, Biblioteca Nazionale Braidense): therein is a reference to

Marc'Antonio Manfredini, who had erected a theatre at Rovigo in 1699 and who is named as the man responsible for that earlier Serenade's commission. This was a very large-scale work, with nine numbers (a concluding chorus of the 'Popoli') in the first part and eleven in the second. In other words a miniature opera some five years before Vivaldi ever composed one.[9]

Vivaldi's relationship with the noble Benedetto Marcello may indeed have been rather strained as a result of the *Teatro*'s publication; but, as we have seen, Alessandro Marcello was now at legal odds with his brother. The whole family however had cordial relations with the famous Borghese family of Rome (who also maintained a palazzo in Venice). Benedetto wrote a Serenata for them (*La morte d'Adone*) in 1719 and had been delivering works to them since 1709. Alessandro dedicated his *Cantate* to Princess Maria Livia Spinola Borghese in 1708, and we can further establish that Alessandro was at Rome in this period because a manuscript is dated 'Roma, 12 maggio 1712'.[10]

Fortunately we can now establish a direct connection between Alessandro Marcello, Vivaldi and the Borghese family in Rome. On 15 October 1722 Alessandro wrote to Princess Maria Livia Spinola Borghese, married since 1691 to Prince Marco Antonio. She was, according to the Italian scholar who discovered this and also Vivaldi's letter, 'the only member of the Borghese family, it seems, with a real passion for music: she was in correspondence with several musicians, in particular with Francesco Gasparini'.[11] Marcello's letter reads as follows:

> Illustrious and most serene Madame,
> I think it is my dearest duty to introduce to your gracious Highness a man whom I much esteem and for whom I profess everlasting gratitude: the person of Sigr. D. Antonio Vivaldi, who is well known to you, a famous professor and violin player who is at the moment in Rome for the opera season during carnival. In receiving my most humble compliments, would you condescend to place him in the shadow of your powerful protection.
> I am very sure that if your Highness would have the graciousness to extend only one ray of that benignity with which you have always favoured my devoted person, he will draw great

advantage from it and I shall add a new reason for obligation to that glory which I believe will remain unchangeable.

I would ask Your Grace most humbly to present my most devoted respects to his Excellency the Prince and Her Excellency Madame, the Duchess of Bracciano.

Venice, 15 October 1722

Your humble and obedient servant
Alessandro Marcello

Ec.^{ma} S. ^{ra} P[ri]n[ci]pe[ss] a Borghese / Roma

Thereupon we have a newly discovered letter from Vivaldi to the Princess after he had returned home, which reads as follows:

Your Excellency,
I lay at the feet of your highest grace my deepest respect and inform you of my happy arrival in Venice, where nothing plagues me except the grief to be no longer in the service of your grace.

If Your Excellency would be kind enough to complete my happiness, it would be sufficient to honour me with one precious command, which would compensate for the pain of being far away. I know only too well that the greatest of problems is my inability, but I pray Your Excellency by your great benignity to overcome that obstacle and honour me with such a command.

Shortly I shall provide the excellent Signora Laura with some music, also Venetian. I humbly beg Your Excellency to allow me to lie at the feet of all the members of your illustrious house and recommend myself with humblest respect.

Your obedient and devoted servant
Antonio Vivaldi

Venice, 20 March 1723

The introduction had led to Vivaldi obtaining an operatic commission from Rome, where in 1723 he produced *Ercole sul Termodonte* at the Teatro Capranica. It was the second opera of the Capranica's season (the theatre was named after its owner-cum-impresario, Federico Capranica), the first having been the rather weak *Oreste* by Benedetto Micheli. It was, in any case, the second carnival opera at Rome that was always considered the more important and for which more lavish sets were constructed and the best singers and composers engaged.

All of a sudden Vivaldi was a popular man in the Eternal City. He was being pitted with success against the younger operatic generation, including such men as Nicolò Porpora (later to be Haydn's teacher) and Leonardo Vinci. Vivaldi's contacts with the Roman aristocracy were assured by the Borghese's protection – including the Pope himself (probably Benedict XIII, who was elected in May 1723). We have this information from Vivaldi himself, in a letter of 23 November 1737 to Bentivoglio (which will be quoted *in extenso* below), wherein the composer tells us that he played the violin in the Vatican. Among the princes and cardinals who had been famous patrons of music since Handel's sojourn at the beginning of the century, Vivaldi was well received by Prince Colonna and by the last and most celebrated of them all, Cardinal Pietro Ottoboni (1667–1740), patron of Arcangelo Corelli and the painter Francesco Trevisani, and an old admirer of Handel's. Ottoboni had always been interested in the Teatro Capranica, and now the famous artist Pier Leone Ghezzi (a member of the Ottoboni circle) sketched the only authentic likeness of Vivaldi, entitled 'Il Prete Rosso Compositor / di musica che fece / L'opera a Capranica del 1723'. He also drew one of Vivaldi's singers, Giacinto Fontana, known as the 'Little Butterfly' ('Farfallino') on 20 January 1723, adding 'che cantò dell'opera del prete rosso nel Teatro Aliberti' (mixing up the Capranica, where Il Farfallino was actually singing, with the rival house).

Vivaldi was invited to participate in the carnival season of 1724 on an even greater scale. The first Capranica opera was *La virtù trionfante degli amori, e degl'odii* for which Benedetto Micheli composed the first, Vivaldi the second and Nicola Romaldo the third acts. The second opera at the Capranica season of 1724 was *Giustino*, entirely by Vivaldi and based on an old drama adapted in 1711 by Pietro Pariati. Later (1737) Handel would also set the Vivaldi text.

In *Giustino* we find the characteristic, so-called 'Lombard rhythm', which much impressed J.J. Quantz, Frederick the Great's flautist, and author, much later, of a famous theoretical treatise (*Versuch einer Anweisung die Flöte traversiere zu spielen*, Berlin

1752). Writing in his autobiography,[12] Quantz records that he arrived at Rome on 11 July 1724. 'What most often reached my ears was the Lombard style. Vivaldi had just introduced it to Rome along with his operas and, in that style, had won the Romans so completely that it was almost as if they could not bear to hear anything except that written in such a manner.' Quantz thereupon elaborates on this particular rhythm, the Scottish snap (as we call it).

Most of the great Ottoboni music library has, alas, perished; but by an extraordinary coincidence, some of it found its way to the Henry Watson Library in Manchester (U.K.). Among the Vivaldian treasures are twelve violin sonatas (RV 754, 755, 756, 17a, 757, 758, 759, 760, 3, 6, 12, 22) with autograph corrections and additions, and two concertos (RV 90, 761). Some of the violin sonatas exist in other versions, so that a comparison may be made. The bass line has been simplified and the violin made more lyrical and operatic in the sense of singing lines.[13]

An equally interesting find from the Ottoboni collection at Manchester is a different, authentic version of *The Four Seasons* from Opus 8, as noted above (p. 68). The Manchester version is about to be published, as I write, in facsimile by the Garland Press in New York, edited by Paul Everett (under the title 'The Manchester Concerto Partbooks').

Thus, Rome occupied a position of central importance in Vivaldi's years of wandering; perhaps the Ottoboni connection – the Cardinal visited Venice in 1726 – is the most important result of the Rome stay, giving us hitherto unknown works and/or arrangements. On all counts Rome must have represented a distinct encouragement for Vivaldi, if indeed the publication of *Il teatro alla moda* was as detrimental to his operatic reputation in Venice as has been largely believed. We may, however, surmise that Vivaldi continued to write works in great quantity for the Pietà – his contract was renewed while he was at Rome – and that with Gasparini's absence, Vivaldi began to concentrate on church music to a much greater extent than hitherto. This period in Vivaldi's life therefore provides a welcome opportunity to discuss this aspect of his art, mostly known to us only in the course of the last few decades of this twentieth century, but of central importance to our understanding of his greatness.

VII
The Church Music

ैल

As we have seen above (p. 37), Gasparini left the Pietà, ostensibly on sick leave, 23 April 1713, but in the event never returned to his post. Among the musicians appointed as 'maestro di coro' in his absence, we may name Pietro dall'Olio (1713–14), Carlo Pietro Grua (1719–d. 1726), Giovanni Porta (1726–37) and Alessandro Porta (1739–41), all of whom evidently turned out to be less than perfect composers of sacred music. As early as 1715, the governing board recognized Vivaldi's merits (see above, p. 38) and listed among the music he had already composed a complete Mass (possibly the work preserved only in Warsaw, but that Mass's authenticity had not yet been established), a Vespers, an oratorio (*Moyses Deus Pharaonis*, 1714) and thirty motets – for which they paid him an *ex gratia* sum of fifty ducats.

Can we reconcile this list with the known extant compositions by Vivaldi? Admittedly he composed a great deal of sacred music after 1715 but can we put together one, or even two, Vespers from the many psalm movements in the Turin collection, and elsewhere? Piero Damilano[1] believes we can, but unfortunately we have had, as far as Vivaldi is concerned, no sensational discovery such as the original performance material for Handel's Roman Vespers which was auctioned by Sotheby's in London in 1985 and which thus resolved the problem whether there was, or was not, a Roman Vespers by Handel in 1707. The problem with Damilano's ingenious solution is that he includes spurious works and also those – such as the *Dixit Dominus* (RV 594) – with male vocal parts of a kind that effectively prohibit their having been performed by the girls at the Pietà. Sometimes, as Michael Talbot[2] reminds us, we are fortunate enough to have the girl soloists of the Pietà listed, as in the setting of

Psalm 147, *Lauda Jerusalem* (RV 609), where two, Margarita and Giulietta, are named as the soprano soloists of the first *coro* and two others, Fortunata and Chiaretta, of the second *coro*. We can even date the piece approximately, since these four girls also sang in *Il coro delle muse*, a Serenata by various composers, including Vivaldi, performed in honour of Frederick Christian, Prince-Elector of Saxony, at the Pietà on 21 March 1740. Since Vivaldi left Venice for good some six weeks later, *Lauda Jerusalem* must have been composed before March 1740.

In the late version of the *Magnificat* there are also Pietà soloists named (see below, p. 89) including Chiaretta in 'Qui fecit', which established this as the final version of this oft-rewritten work. What is distinctly puzzling is the presence of bass voice(s) in the choral parts of those pieces obviously destined for the Pietà such as the *Lauda Jerusalem* and the late *Magnificat*. It has been suggested that there were probably enough low contralto voices to sing the tenor parts, but I refuse to accept the idea that they sang the bass parts transposed an octave higher. Why write any bass parts at all for a female choir? Even if Vivaldi intended to sell his Pietà pieces elsewhere – and we know he frequently did – this seems a specious argument at best. If Vivaldi conducted the choir, this fact presupposes that men were not literally forbidden in the choir-loft. Perhaps bass-voiced members of the church personnel came in to sing them. I believe that the last word on this subject has yet to be said.

Having established that most of Vivaldi's sacred music has now been accurately dated by Talbot,[3] I give a list of what I believe to be his finest available church pieces in Appendix VI. What follows are comments about the most outstanding of them, destined for the layman rather than the musicologist, who will wish to consult the specialist literature. Numbers in square brackets refer to the list in Appendix VI.

Some of Vivaldi's major surviving pieces of church music are parts of the Mass: *Kyrie*, *Gloria* and *Credo*. North of the Alps these would normally be fairly short, unified compositions (e.g. Mozart's Kyries, including the late period K 341) but in Italy in Vivaldi's time it was fashionable to give them several movements each. The splendid

Kyrie in G minor (RV 587) [1], for instance, has three movements, beginning with a substantial orchestral introduction. Two of these movements were (later?) borrowed for the remarkable Concerto in D minor for strings (RV 129) with the curious title *Il Madrigalesco* ('The Madrigalesque'). This was music Vivaldi loved and evidently thought highly of, for we find it as well in the relatively early *Credo* (RV 591) in E minor [4].

Of the two extant settings of the *Gloria*, the earlier one in D (RV 588) [2] is the less known, largely because it was published later than RV 589. It is scored for two oboes, one trumpet, strings and organ continuo, with a choir of sopranos, altos, tenors and basses. It is preceded by an Introduction (a recitative and aria for contralto, a very florid and brilliant piece). If the opening Chorus is not as spectacular as RV 589, it is none the less arresting, with a brilliant entry for the trumpet. The following Largo, 'Et in terra pax', is an extraordinary movement. Vivaldi obviously considered peace on earth to be at best a fragile achievement, and both settings are remarkable for their serious, even tragic mood. The sighing vocal lines, walking slowly down the scale, are grippingly effective and the whole is a vast panorama, developed slowly and with a certain awed respect.

The delicate and graceful duet of the 'Laudamus' contains some rapturous passages for the two ladies in thirds, and some attractive vocal imitations, while the following 'Gratias agimus' is a slow-moving choral movement with equally slow-moving harmonic patterns and impressive block choral writing. In the 'Domine Deus', the oboe part is extremely difficult, especially if we recall the primitive instrument for which Vivaldi was writing at that time. The duet is delightful and was obviously intended to establish the following central number in this work. The central part of this *Gloria*, on which Vivaldi has caused the full weight of his inspiration to fall, is the 'Qui tollis'; and as so often in the sacred music, it is a slow movement, with the composer's matchless paced choral entries securely placed in a thick but at the same time lucid texture. There is a solo oboe part, sparsely and effectively used. Next comes the 'Qui sedes', where the rapturous string writing (often played in performance as solo parts) is especially beautiful as an accompaniment to the contralto solo. This is perhaps the place to say that

Vivaldi has made a speciality of the contralto voice, no doubt influenced by the presence of so many in the Pietà, though it is impossible to say if this beautiful *Gloria* was actually composed for the Pietà, at least in its present state.

The 'Quoniam' begins with a rarity – a wind band solo, to prepare for a jolly soprano solo with amazingly difficult passage work.

This *Gloria* ends, like its companion RV 589, with a reworking of a 'Gloria' fugue on the same text by G.H. Ruggieri, but with a notable addition in the form of a trumpet solo.

The enormous popularity of the second *Gloria* in D (RV 589) [3] derives, most probably, from two important factors: (1) It was one of the first pieces of Vivaldian sacred music to be performed at the Chiesa dei Servi, as part of the *Settimana Celebretiva di Antonio Vivaldi*, produced by the Accademia Musicale Chigiana in Siena in September 1939; on that occasion, the pieces were selected and conducted by Alfredo Casella, who also edited all the church music performed. Casella even wrote the programme notes, and the whole concert was broadcast by the Italian Radio E.I.A.R. It was also the occasion at which the *Credo* in E minor (RV 591) the *Stabat Mater* (RV 621) and the Motet 'O qui coeli' (RV 631) for soprano and orchestra with basso continuo (organ) were heard for the first time in 200 years. The *Gloria* was also the first major piece of Vivaldian church music to be recorded, shortly after World War II. (2) The second factor, and the decisive one, is quite simply that this *Gloria* is possibly the most accessible and immediately comprehensible of all Vivaldi's sacred music – the *Four Seasons* of its genre.

The beginning, with its octave leaps in the strings and the subsequent run with the trumpet, has become synonymous with the festive brilliance of Vivaldi's church music. It exerts an almost hypnotic sense of forward drive in the listener and must have electrified the congregation in its time.

The subtle key scheme of both *Glorias* shows how cleverly Vivaldi has used the central key of D major – the trumpet key *par excellence* of eighteenth century Italy. It is here employed only for the beginning and the end. Casella was right to single out the moving and broadly conceived 'Et in terra pax hominibus' which, 'contrary to what the words might lead one to expect, is a piece suffused with profound sadness.'[4] After a gay and light-hearted duet for two sopranos ('Laudamus te'), there follow two movements in E minor, the 'Gratias' and a magnificent fugal 'Domine Deus propter magnam'. The 'Domine Deus' is a dialogue between solo soprano and a meltingly – indeed hauntingly – beautiful oboe solo (which is sometimes played by the solo violin, since in the autograph manuscript Vivaldi specifies 'Violino solo o oboe solo'). This section is a Largo in the form of a *siciliano*, with pizzicato lower strings.

There is, in this exceptional work, not only one movement of monumental greatness but two: after the astonishingly vast horizons of 'Et in terra pax hominibus', we now have another slow movement of large density – the duet between contralto solo and choir in the 'Domine Deus, agnus Dei' which reminded Casella of the finale of Beethoven's Ninth Symphony.

The 'Quoniam tu solus sanctus' uses the material of the opening 'Gloria', and the 'Cum Sancto Spiritu' gives us yet another version of the much-maligned fugue by G.M. Ruggieri, completely rewritten (with dashing trumpet solos) by Vivaldi, 'which concludes in a dignified way this stupendous Vivaldian masterpiece, without doubt one of the most important discoveries of this *Settimana*', wrote Alfredo Casella in his notes to the 1939 programme.

The *Credo* in E minor (RV 591) [4] has four sections. The first is an Allegro chorus with the orchestral introduction (alternating quavers and semi-quavers) carried through the movement with appropriate intervals in between. The bass line runs in nervous quavers such as Haydn was to use so effectively later in the century (and we must recall that among the music catalogued at Eisenstadt is *The Four Seasons*). The choir is employed in blocks of harmonic patterns, reciting the words.

The second movement, Adagio, is the 'Et incarnatus est', with remarkable harmonic surprises ('et homo factus est') and dramatic pauses. The third, Largo, is the 'Crucifixus' in masterly polyphonic layout, with imitational entries. It is a long and intricate section, with chromatic writing at Vivaldi's most daring. There is a particularly impressive harmonic twist at the word 'passus et sepultus est'.

The fourth and final movement uses, as Vivaldi loves to do, the material of the opening Allegro, which then leads to a fugal section on a *cantus firmus* in long notes countered by a rapid countersubject (to set forth the words 'Et vitam venturi saeculi, amen'). It is a stern, impressive and slightly forbidding *Credo*: we should not forget that Vivaldi had a very austere side to his complicated and multi-faceted nature.

The second main category of Vivaldi's church music is his settings of Psalms, of which certain favourites, such as Psalm 109 ('Dixit Dominus') and 111 ('Beatus vir') were set more than once. It was not uncommon for every group of words or phrases to be made into a separate movement, with contrasting singers and instrumentation.

The large-scale 'Dixit Dominus' (RV 594) [5] begins with a quick movement for the assembled forces, with trumpet parts cutting through the texture. One notes the use of a *cantus firmus* technique, as well as the usual block choral entries – there is constant diversity in the texture.

The second movement is another chorus, with a dotted orchestral introduction which continues and provides the backbone of the whole sound. Again, there is a fine differentiation in the choral writing between blocks of sound, imitative entries and unison endings. In the 'Tecum Principium' one notes the unfailingly effective use Vivaldi makes of the chest notes, the lower register of this kind of voice, which creates a special, unforgettable sound. This is followed by a chorus with cascades of choral sound, moving to a quicker tempo with contrapuntal intricacy. At the end there is yet another impressive use of the *cantus firmus* technique.

It is the sixth section ('Dominus a dextris tuis') which renders it highly unlikely that this work was intended for the Pietà. Vivaldi sets the music out as if he were writing an instrumental concerto, and after the very concerto-like ritornello, the voices are used as if they were part of the instrumental operation. The vocal writing is extraordinarily florid.

The next section is dominated by spectacularly difficult trumpet parts, one in each coro, imitating each other as they each race up the D major scale to their top d''', illustrating the text: 'He shall sit in judgement over the heathen. He shall bring about destruction. He shall strike down heads in many lands'. This is followed by 'De torrente', with waves of arpeggios sliding upwards (illustrating the 'brook by the wayside'): more delightfully descriptive music. The

Chorus now returns to the opening music to illustrate the Doxology that follows, where we find again the *cantus firmus* manner which we, possibly quite wrongly, associate with the north – the melody, well known in Germany, was used by Bach at the beginning of the 'Goldberg' Variations (BWV 988). This is music of huge complexity in which difficult contrapuntal problems are posed and instantly solved with Venetian dexterity. This 'Dixit Dominus' is an undoubted masterpiece.

Because of the indispensable male sections, it is considered unlikely that the large and splendid setting of Psalm 111, 'Beatus vir', in C (RV 597) [6] was performed at the Pietà, at least in this version. Michael Talbot thinks such works might have been for the Venetian Convent of San Lorenzo, which annually imported groups of musicians for festive occasions. This is another striking setting of the text, with variations of tempo and instruments to reinforce each phrase.

The beginning is used cleverly by Vivaldi as a kind of refrain which he brings back at the end of nearly every section: he calls this 'Antifona'. The first choral entry of this particular movement, with its long notes soaring over the orchestra, is striking and beautiful. The 'Potens in terra' is another instance of Vivaldi's famous – to some, in those days, infamous – use of unison choral writing, sometimes doubled by the orchestra, but an effective way to illustrate the text.

For the fourth section, 'Exortum est in tenebris', Vivaldi writes a gently homophonic choral movement, later expertly 'broken up' into patterns and entries – spread, as it were, into counterpoint. 'Jucundus homo' is an aria for soprano and continuo. There is a solo organ part, a rarity in Vivaldi which, however, seems to have been a tradition at the Pietà: we find it in *Judith* (see below). Again, a concerto-like opening, after which the soprano takes over as if she were a second instrument in a double concerto. Next comes a chorus on 'In memoria aeterna', with quiet string entries in imitation, like a great slow movement of a concerto from *L'estro armonico*. As in the 'Et misericordia' from the *Magnificat* and *Gloria* settings, this finely fashioned movement is central to the work, with its fugal subtleties and intricate contrapuntal dexterity. Another chorus, 'Paratum cor ejus', has a striking orchestral part that sets off the unison choral writing. We are once again reminded of Handel's use of *cantus firmus* during his Roman period, here with the divided chorus, the orchestra binding everything together.

The aria for tenor and orchestra 'Peccator videbit' has some brilliantly original surprises in the orchestral part, a sudden burst of speed, etc. The tenor's part is extremely difficult technically. Finally comes the chorus 'Gloria patri', with a return, as usual, to the material of the beginning to illustrate the words of the Doxology. The words 'Et in saecula saeculorum' is a stretto fugue, with highly unexpected effects, once more using the *cantus firmus* technique so well known to us from Handel's *Dixit Dominus* of Rome, 1707. In the Vivaldi setting there is an incredible pedal point on the dominant at the end, which creates a great sense of suspense, thankfully resolved by the brief cadence.

Another setting of the same Psalm, 'Beatus vir', in B flat (RV 598) [7] begins with a long string orchestral introduction which seems to prepare us for a concerto, but this time it is for three solo voices: first the contralto, then two soprano soloists together ('Potens in terra') followed, after another ritornello, by the first choral entry ('Gloria et divitiae in domo ejus'). More and more the structure begins to sound like a concerto. The pattern is repeated: alto solo ('Ex ortum est in tenebris'), ritornello, two soprano soli ('Jucundus homo'), ritornello, chorus ('In memoria aeterna'); ritornello, alto solo ('Paratum cor ejus'), ritornello, two soprano soli ('Dispersit') – cleverly this time, because of the text, they do not begin together but enter after one another, ritornello, chorus ('Peccator videbit'); ritornello, alto solo ('Gloria Patri'), two soprano soli together ('Sicut erat in principio'), naturally with the same music as their first entry. This time there is no ritornello afterwards: the chorus plunges in with its 'Amen'. One is astonished to see the total transformation of the Baroque (Vivaldian) ritornello form of the concerto into this terse and formally perfect piece of sacred music.

The 'Laudate pueri' in G (RV 601) [8] has several slow arias, the first stately and radiant. The 'Gloria Patri' contains a very idiomatic flute movement and there is a florid and racy conclusion with boisterous string parts.

Another setting of the same Psalm (RV 602) [9] has one of Vivaldi's bright and optimistic beginnings, later revised, and continues with the music closely shadowing the words. In 'A solis ortu usque ad occasum' he uses canonic devices to illustrate the rising sun in a movement of peculiar beauty and simplicity, while 'Suscitans a terra' is a warlike duet with fierce dotted accompaniment. The longest movement in the whole work and its central point is the 'Quis sicut Dominus', a sober and beautiful aria; 'Gloria Patri' is an extended oboe solo, in duet with the first solo soprano.

The 'Laudate Dominum', in D minor (RV 606) [10], coming from his early years, is a short masterpiece, with strange chromatic lines, dominated by a first and second (unison) violin line of hypnotic compulsion, similar to the Credo setting in E minor (RV 591), discussed above.

The 'Nisi Dominus' in G minor (RV 608) [12] has another concerto-like beginning with a tersely rhythmic part for the strings. The vocal line is of a brilliance which, if well sung, is totally captivating. Again, Vivaldi uses the ritornello to space his vocal entries. The next movement is a continuo aria in a slow-moving and flowing vocal line. The presto interruptions are as dramatic as an operatic scene. One of two centrally important slow movements in this unusual Psalm setting is the 'Cum dederit'. Here we have another example of Vivaldi's 'night music', as in the dog-barking scene in *The Four Seasons* or in one of the concertos entitled *La Notte*, such as that for bassoon (RV 501). The repeated dotted figures at this slow tempo and the dream-like quality of the contralto solo's line are intended to describe the peace that descends on those who love the Lord. It is a magical and touching movement, especially the slow, upwards-moving chromatic lines in the middle and towards the end.

In the next continuo aria the sudden entry of the strings, towards the middle, creates a vivid effect.

The piece ends with 'Gloria Patri'. As with those altarpieces with an angel playing a string instrument as if it were totally outside the action of the panel itself, Vivaldi introduces a silvery solo for the viola d'amore (an instrument with sympathetic vibrating strings, which the composer may have played himself). The praise for the Holy Trinity appears like some marvellous dream, a trance of beauty. This must be a highpoint in the whole of Vivaldi's music.

We end, as usual, with the same music as the beginning

(Doxology), to which a soberly brilliant 'Amen' (movement IX) has been deftly added as an additional movement (the strings have a peculiarly effective little ritornello figure in the concluding section).

In the late-period work 'Lauda Jerusalem' (RV 609) [13] there is a little figure which returns to haunt us, not only because it is striking in itself but because it reappears (without the trills and with the second, fourth etc., notes a third lower) in Mozart:

We do not suggest, however, that Mozart heard or even saw the music of this Psalm when he visited northern Italy, but it is interesting that this kind of phrase is part of a great Vivaldian tradition. This 'Lauda Jerusalem' is worked out in several different combinations: 1) Two choirs and two orchestras, in other words the famous old Venetian effect of *cori spezzati*, which Vivaldi could have used at the Pietà or anywhere else; 2) first solo and first orchestra; 3) second solo and second orchestra. There are ten sections which are treated like a concerto's ritornello form, viz. Verses 1, 4, 7 and 10 are orchestral and choral tutti, while Verses 2, 3, 5, 6 and 8–9 (joined) have first and second sopranos, with florid and difficult coloratura parts. All, like the previously discussed *Credo* in E minor, is bound together by the orchestral ritornelli – another scintillating exercise in structural unity and nervous inspiration. In Vivaldi's autograph (Turin) the composer has noted the names of two sopranos for each solo part, i.e. four names. Whether this means that two voices should sing each solo part, or whether they are alternate suggestions, is not clear.

Of the *Magnificat* in G Minor (RV 610) [14] there are, as Michael Talbot has now established, three basic versions: (1) the original, composed between 1713 and 1717, with an orchestration of strings and continuo (organ), and with a high vocal bass part, hence possibly sung by a Pietà contralto; (2) a new version for Cardinal Pietro Ottoboni in Rome, to whose office of the Cancelleria was attached the church of S. Lorenzo in Damaso. Oboes were added and the vocal bass line moved downwards to accommodate normal male voices. In Vivaldi's autograph (Turin) the work was now marked to indicate the use of two *cori*, i.e. the forces were divided to produce antiphonal effects. This second version has been recorded on the Hyperion label with notes by Michael Talbot, including material not in his brilliant little book, so often consulted here; (3) in 1739 Vivaldi wrote a third version, again for the Pietà, with replacement of three movements by five new ones for solo singers at the Pietà, whose names are recorded:

> Et exsultavit per l'Apollonia
> Qui respexit per la Bolognesa
> Qui fecit per la Chiaretta
> Esurientes per l'Ambrosina
> Sicut locutus est per l'Abetta

This version has been recorded under the supervision of Abbé Carl de Nys for Lumen-Schwann.

The *Magnificat* is characterized by the monumental style of its chorus, the originality and daring qualities of its modulations, and its chromatic harmonies. As always, there is the omnipresent influence of the concerto, both in some of the general structures as well as in the use of concerto-like ritornelli. In the second version, Verses 2–4 (the words 'Et exsultavit', 'Qui respexit' and 'Qui fecit', later turned into three separate arias) are assigned to three different solo singers – soprano, alto, tenor – with choral interjections. The 'Et misericordia' is the centrally important, massively grand choral moment which may reflect a study of 'De Torrente' in Handel's Roman *Dixit Dominus* of 1707. Vivaldi could easily have seen or studied this amazing production of Handel's youth either at the library of its commissioner, Cardinal Carlo Colonna (1665–1739) or at Cardinal Ottoboni's. In this 'Et misericordia' there are endlessly novel twists of harmony.

'Fecit potentiam in brachio suo' ('He hath showed strength with His Arm. He hath scattered the proud in the imagination of their hearts. He hath put down the mighty from their seats, and exalted them of low degree'): the first part is illustrated by vigorous string motifs, followed by the devastating effect of choral and instrumental unisons ('Deposuit potentes'), continuing for bar after bar, to the very end of this section. Vivaldi has found a startling contrast to illuminate the next section on poverty, 'Esurientes implevit' ('He hath filled the hungry with good things and the rich He hath sent empty away').

For the Doxology, we have now come to expect a repeat of the opening music for 'Sicut erat in principio' ('As it was in the beginning, is now and ever shall be, world without end. Amen'); and we look forward to, and receive with interest, a grand fugue at the work's conclusion.

It is curious that the dignified and beautiful *Salve Regina* (RV 616) [15] has never achieved the popularity of the *Stabat Mater* (see below), although it provides a magnificent vehicle for a contralto voice with spectacular chest notes. But the vocal part also requires considerable flexibility (as in the middle of the opening section). The Ricordi edition suppresses the recorder parts, as noted above, and indicates transverse flutes only. There are also many dubious suggestions (mutes in the first movement's second orchestra?).

There is another setting (RV 617 in F major) of the *Salve Regina* – Vivaldi composed three of these Marian antiphons – which has survived only in the contemporary MS. parts in the Moravian Library at Brno (Brünn), in former Czechoslovakia, but which has been recorded recently (Philips 432 088–2). It is shorter – there are only four movements – and is distinguished by a pretty violin solo in two of these movements.

In the *Stabat Mater* in F minor (RV 621) [16], of central importance to the comprehension of Vivaldi's music, the formal scheme is of a devastatingly effective simplicity: movements 1, 3, 4, 6–9 in F minor, while nos. 2 and 5 are in C minor. The music of the first three movements is moreover repeated in the fourth to sixth movements. The 'Eia mater', 'Fac, ut ardet' and the 'Amen' are newly composed.

The text, of characteristically Franciscan spirituality, was hitherto attributed to Jacopo de Benedetti (*c.* 1220–1306); but recent research now suggests that the poem was actually written by the 'doctor seraphicus' Saint Bonaventura, a Franciscan cardinal (1221–74) who was the spiritual leader of the Friars Minor. Vivaldi

set the first ten of twenty stanzas – composers usually set all twenty
and the 'Amen' (Pergolesi, Alessandro Scarlatti, Haydn). All twenty
with the 'Amen' are used when the *Stabat Mater* is inserted into the
Ordinary of the Mass as a sequence, but Rome also allowed the
Stabat to be sung as a Vesper hymn in reduced form at the two feasts
of the Seven Dolours of the Blessed Virgin Mary (15 September and
the Friday before Good Friday). Abbé Carl de Nys dates the music
on the basis of the Vatican's decree regarding the *Stabat Mater's*
introduction as 'prose' or 'sequence' ('testo o sequenza') into the
Catholic liturgy, i.e. the late summer of 1727. Recently Michael
Talbot has dated the work to 1711, relating it to Vivaldi's visit to
Brescia in that year for the Feast of the Purification of the Blessed
Virgin at the Chiesa della Pace, which had at its disposal a highly
paid male alto as well as a small string group (four violins, cello,
double bass) and organ.

This is the most sombre setting of the *Stabat* known to Western
music – formally, an impeccable construction, emotionally as bleak
as a Grünewald Passion. We have noted Vivaldi's remarkable
knowledge of, and affection for, the contralto voice; he understands
the darker side of the timbre and here he puts it to constant and very
moving use. But above and beyond all this is the extraordinary sense
of spirituality and profound sadness behind this uncompromising
music in what would be Haydn's favourite key of F minor – Seven
Dolours indeed! Vivaldi was above everything else a priest in the
Holy Roman Catholic Church, and this music is a great declaration
of faith.

Finally let us look at a few of Vivaldi's sacred motets, which
illustrate his ability to create whole tone-poems round a particular
text. 'In furore giustissimae irae' (RV 626) [18] is a solo motet for
soprano and strings. By now, we have come to expect the intensely
rhythmic, concerto-like opening, which leads off the customary four
sections in which Vivaldi generally wrote these: 1) first da capo aria
in C minor with a middle section in G minor; 2) recitative; 3) a largo
da capo aria with a middle part which moves from B flat to C minor;
4) concluding Alleluja. Note the incredible sense of forward drive,
largely engendered by the relentless repeated quavers in the bass
line, for which the angry text is largely responsible.

The text of 'In turbata mare irato' (RV 627) [19] suggested to Vivaldi another scene of vivid *Ton-malerei*, or word-painting: the racing tremolo strings conjure up the stormy seas. As before, there are two da capo arias framing a recitative and the final Alleluja. In the second movement, the recitative has the words 'Splende serena, o lux amata' ('Shine serene, dearest light') which is of course a reference to the Virgin, as is the text of the second (slow) aria, 'Resplende, bella divina stella' ('Shine forth, beautiful divine star'). The final Alleluja is skittish and angular with very odd modulations and excursions into strange keys.

In 'Invicti bellate' (RV 627) [20], a military atmosphere is conjured up by the strings, and then the soprano, imitating trumpet fanfares – a hark-back to the Venetian tone-painting of Claudio Monteverdi in his famous and seminal *Combattimento di Tancredi e Clorinda*. The recitative 'Fortes estote in bello' ('Be brave in war') is followed by a larghetto da capo aria ('Jesus, our eternal Lord, give strength to my heart'), a pensive and quiet contrast to the belligerent beginning and end of the motet. The final Alleluja has the dramatic coloratura writing that befits a war-like subject.

In 'Nulla in mundo pax sincera' for soprano, strings and organ continuo (RV 630) [21], the subject is peace, and for the opening we have an E major *siciliano*-like aria with a middle section in the (for those days) rather rare key of C sharp minor. After the recitative there is a second aria with an even bolder modulatory scheme: A major (Allegro), modulating in the middle part from C sharp minor to the daringly rare key of F sharp minor (only one symphony in the whole of the eighteenth century, Haydn's No. 45 ['Farewell'], is known to have been in this key). The Alleluja is the usual coloratura set-piece, returning to the home key of E major. An instructive lesson on how to compose a work celebrating peace as compared to the furious rage of the C minor Motet 'In furore giustissimae irae'.

I believe that Vivaldi's sacred music is at the core and centre of his artistic thought; that the real *prete rosso* is the man who composed these extraordinary pieces, illustrating the whole of human emotions, and also man faced with divinity. There is Vivaldi's deep veneration for the Blessed Virgin Mary, as we have seen many times, especially in the sorrowful *Stabat Mater*. There is moreover the sense of divine power, even to the Last Judgement-like sound of the trumpets in 'Judicabit in nationibus' from the *Dixit Dominus*. Finally there is his sense of awe, faced with the dubious prospect of 'Et in terra pax hominibus' from the two *Glorias* – perhaps the most original setting of such words in the eighteenth century.

Probably this corpus of works reflects the tenor of Vivaldi's sacred music more effectively that the Oratorio *Judith* which was, in the 1950's, the one work by the composer in this genre known to most of the general public. *Judith* has its moments of greatness, but it suffers from the same loquacity as do the operas; yet the work utilizes a brilliant and diverse orchestration, with all manner of exotic instruments such as chalumeau and clarinets, as well as mandolin, solo organ, five *viole all'inglese* (another viola with even more sympathetic vibrating strings then the viola d'amore, also included in *Judith*), trumpets and kettledrums. Until we knew the *Magnificat* and the *Stabat Mater*, or 'Nisi Dominus', *Judith* was no mean representative of Vivaldi in the church. But now I think we have more, and better, ambassadors to represent this central part of Vivaldi's *oeuvre*. I have said before that I very much doubt the ability of Vivaldi's operas to hold the stage at the end of our twentieth century, and beyond. On the other hand, I think that his sacred music will soon be regarded as the equal of, if not in many respects superior to, the instrumental music for which he has always, and rightly, been so highly regarded.

VIII
Patrons, Travels and the Giraud Sisters

꠸

The Biblioteca Marciana in Venice owns a manuscript volume of letters by Abbé Antonio Conti to a French lady, Madame de Caylus; and it is from this rich source, first mined by the indefatigable Marc Pincherle and later by Remo Giazotto,[1] that we learn of the fortunes of Antonio Vivaldi and his star pupil, Anna Giraud (or Girò), now appearing in San Angelo, the directorship of which Vivaldi had now effectively reassumed. In the autumn of 1725 it was *L'inganno trionfante in amore*, adapted by an interesting literary and musical *dilettante*, G.M. Ruggieri, whose fugue for a *Gloria* Vivaldi had shamelessly, but possibly with the knowledge of the composer, pillaged for the conclusion of his two *Gloria* settings (see above, p. 82). There followed no fewer than three operas for the Carnival and Autumn season of San Angelo: *Cunegonda*, *La fede tradita e vendicata* and *Dorilla in Tempe*. This was followed, in 1727, by *Medea e Giasone*, *Farnace*, *Orlando* and *Rosilena ed Oronta*; while in this incredible year, Vivaldi also composed two operas for non-Venetian venues, *Ipermestra* for the Teatro della Pergola in Florence and *Siroe, rè di Persia* for Reggio Emilia, the latter from a libretto by Metastasio himself. Here is the cast for the successful *Farnace*, performed at the Carnival *and* autumn season of 1727.

ATTORI

Farnace Re di Ponto *La Sig: Maria Maddalena Pieri. Virtuosa del Seren. Duca di Modona [sic]*.
Berenice Regina di Cappadocia Madre di Tamiri *La Sig. Angela Capuano Romana detta la Capuanina*

Tamiri, Regina Sposa di Farnace *La Sig. Anna Girò*
Selinda Sorella di Farnace *La Sig. Lucrezia Baldini*
Pompeo Pro-Console Romano nell'Asia *Il Sig. Lorenzo Moretti*
Gilade Principe del Sangue Reale, e Capitano di Berenice *Il
  Sig. Filippo Finazzi*
Aquilio Prefetto delle Legioni Romane *Il Sig. Domenico
  Gioseppe Galletti*
Un Fanciullo Figlio di Farnace, e Tamiri.
    Il Luogo dell'Azione in Eraclea.
    Cori di Soldati Romani, e Asiatici
    La Musica e del celebre Sig. D. Antonio Vivaldi Maestro
        di Cappella di S.A.S. il Signor Principe Filippo
        Langravio d'Hassia D'armstath [*sic*]
Li Balli sono invenzioni del Sig. Giovanni Galletto:

On 23 February 1727, Abbé Conti writes: 'Vivaldi has written three operas in less than three months, two for Venice and the third for Florence; the latter has re-established the theatre in that city and made him a great deal of money.' About Giraud he writes, without mentioning her name:

> ... The new opera at San Grisostomo [*sic*] was more successful than the previous one, because of the magnificence of the decorations, but the composition is so detestable and the music so sad that I slept through one act. My opera is the new one at San Angelo. The libretto is passable if you overlook the mistakes of one episode which is quite contrary to reality. The music is by Vivaldi, it is very varied both in its sublime and tender moments; his pupil performed miracles even if her voice is not one of the most beautiful.

When Anna Giraud was making her debut during the Carnival season of 1725, she attracted the attention of Alderano IV Cybo, Duke of Massa, who proceeded to present her with the handsome sum of sixty zecchini. Anna was looking for a good and reliable harpsichord and her attention was drawn to one, which included a four-foot stop (i.e. an octave higher than the normal register, called the eight-foot), and had been built by the famous Domenico da

95

Pesaro. Vivaldi supervised the operation and a middleman, one
Giovanni Gallo, was engaged to purchase the instrument from the
owner, Andrea Bonazza, for the price of thirty zecchini. But shortly
after Giraud had acquired the instrument, the previous owner,
Bonazza, heard of the Duke's present of sixty zecchini and seems to
have believed that the whole sum had been intended for Giraud's
future harpsichord. He therefore accused Vivaldi of misappropria-
tion before the relevant magistrature, the Consoli de' Mercanti. The
letter of accusation has not survived, but Vivaldi's defence, drawn
up by one Antonio Signoretti, was recently discovered and is here
presented complete in translation:[2]

Invented chimeras, fanciful inventions, are those disseminated in
this document, presented to this excellent magistrate by Don
Andrea Bonazza, this 27th August of this year against Don
Antonio Vivaldi, while it is false that I have ever asked or
pretended (protecting my station and my occupation) any
percentage deriving from the sale of his harpsichord with a four-
foot register to Signora Anna Girò, virtuoso lady singer; wrong
that H.H. the Duke of Massa Carrara has ever dealt with or
possessed the above mentioned harpsichord, and even more false
that 60 zecchini were handed out or paid by the Duke for the
purchase of the same.

May this man be more considered about the injustice of his
reckless pretensions, the impact of his damning slanders and,
reflecting the real facts with which I intended to justify myself, he
should retract this unbelievable presentation or I will be
acquitted and absolved by the court with solemn protest against
the contents *salvis et in expensis* proposing *quatenus et cetera* in
the following paragraphs.

1 It was and is true that some months before last March Signor
Andrea Bonazza wanted to sell his harpsichord with four-foot
register constructed by Domenico da Pesaro, receiving the same
price or even less.

2 H.H. the Duke of Massa Carrara left Venice on the second of
last March.

3 Immediately after I, Antonio Vivaldi, was given 60 zecchini by
Count Angello Savioli, which I consigned as commissioned by the

above mentioned Duke to the above mentioned Signora Anna
Girò, virtuoso lady singer.
4 It was Signor Giovanni Gallo, mediator, who confirmed the
sale of the above mentioned harpsichord with Signor Bonazza for
30 zecchini, including five for his mediation, because he had to go
at various times to the house of the vendor, to make sure he would
be satisfied and he said various times: yes.
5 The 30 zecchini, the price of the sale, were given to Signor
Giovanni Gallo by Signora Anna Girrò [*sic*].
6 The above mentioned harpsichord was, immediately after the
sale was concluded, taken to the house of the above mentioned
Signora Anna in the contrada Santa Maria Formosa, where it still
is.
1725, the day of September 17th.

This present answer was submitted by the excellent Antonio
Signoretti, go-between of, and in the name of, Reverend Don
Antonio Vivaldi to the excellent Magistrate of the Consuls of the
Merchants.
Belongs to the presentation of Don Andrea Bonazza.
416 [in the margin]
[Venezia, Archivio di Stato, *Consoli dei mercanti*, busta 140, of
that date.]

Since there was patently no foundation in the accusation, the
matter seems to have quietly dropped. But it was, no doubt, the
beginning of a faintly scandalous connection between Vivaldi and
the Giraud sisters.

In 1726 the new Neapolitan Ambassador at the *Serenissima*,
Zuanne Zuccato, wrote to his government as follows:[3]

Here one goes very little to the theatre or to concerts, it's just as
with us, one makes love all day long. No one enjoys a grand
education but everyone sings and there are fine voices which are
naturally exceptional, also that of Annina from the Pietà who is
now creating a furore at all the best theatres, namely at S.
Angelo, and she has no equals as was shown last year at S. Moisè.
Here they sing and play in boats, which are not like ours where
there is open sea, and many here have sails and they give many

balls with singers, both men and women, also on the squares at all hours …

Here, then, is established that 'Annina from the Pietà' is patently the Anna Giraud or Girò, Vivaldi's pupil and protegée. Giazotto[4] gives us also another, more sinister document of the year 1729 from the archives of the Holy Inquisition at Venice, denouncing 'Giuseppi Ciachhi, tenor and musician who lives in the *contrada* di Sant'Angelo in the *Calle della Madona* opposite Modesto Zenche …'. The denunciator was one Zuane Corbi or Corvi and as a witness 'L'Anna che canta alla Pietà ('Anna who sings at the Pietà') was cited. It seems that Anna Giraud was not more than twenty or twenty-two years old at the time. Certainly, she was a very proper young lady, entirely *sans reproche*, because the authorities kept a watchful eye on the girls at the Pietà, some of whom were certainly not *sans reproche*. Take the following document from the files of Vatican secret agents.[5]

Anzola Trevisana, known as *La Galinera*, a prostitute, who lives in the *contrada* Sant'Aponal, at the *traghetto de la Madonetta*, plies her trade on holidays, setting an example which is deplorable and scandalous without in the least enquiring whether it is allowed. Christians and Jews frequent her house, and through the mistresses of the Pietà, who act as procurators, the girls of that Hospital are frequently brought in. They stay there for whole days at a time, in company with a certain Laura, who lives in a house next to that of *la* Trevisana. This Laura is an old courtesan who, now that she has reached a certain age, acts as a procuress.

G B Manuzzi
9 September 1740

Of course the document is fifteen years later than our period, but it is still during Vivaldi's relationship with the Pietà; and it suggests that it would have been rather unlikely for Vivaldi to be carrying on an open affair with Anna Giraud. In fact it would have never entered our heads were it not for the famous correspondence between Vivaldi and Bentivoglio, wherein (on 16 November 1737) we read that Tomaso Ruffo, the Cardinal of Ferrara, refused Vivaldi permission to enter the town, citing Vivaldi's refusal to say Mass and his friendship with Anna Girò (the Italianized spelling). In that same letter Vivaldi states 'fourteen years ago [i.e. 1723] we went together [Vivaldi and the Giraud sisters] to a good many European cities ... I have spent three Carnival Seasons at Rome for the opera ... I have been called to Vienna ...' (see below, p. 149, for the complete letter).

Certainly, Anna Giraud and her sister lived at Vivaldi's house, as we shall learn from one of two famous documents by Carlo Goldoni cited in Chapter X. Remo Giazotto[6] found another interesting document from the files of the Inquisition in Venice. This time the spy, one Giovanni Gilli, was reporting on a grand *souper* given by the Spanish Ambassador to the *Serenissima* to celebrate the marriage of the Infante Philip to Princess Marie-Louise-Elisabeth of France on 26 August 1739. Therein we read that there was music 'by the singer who lives at the house of *abbate* Vivaldi, called la Girò and at the harpsichord sat the *abbate* who indicated the tempo to the instruments which were not many but all excellent in both the vocal and instrumental departments. The music went on until three o'clock in the morning, and then everybody went home ...'.

Soon after Anna had moved into Vivaldi's house, the other sister Paolina (Paulina) joined the establishment, apparently as a nurse for the constantly ailing 'red priest'. Now all this does not necessarily constitute that which many biographers would like to imagine, a jolly *menage à trois*. It *might* have been that, of course; and indeed Anna Giraud *may* have been Vivaldi's mistress. But I think it unlikely that the Inquisition would have ignored such a situation, and it is not enough, in my opinion, to base such a relationship on what the Cardinal of Ferrara thought. Ruffo had a reputation for being something of a martinet and a prude: he actually forbade the clergy in his diocese to take part in the Carnival festivities of 1738, a year before the famous anti-Vivaldian edict. We shall have to leave the Giraud sisters as we find them in the documents: Anna a successful singer and protegée of Vivaldi's, possibly (*dixit* Giazotto) also his secretary and possibly his mistress; together with Paolina, probably Vivaldi's nurse and possibly also his mistress.

But before we leave the curious history of the Giraud sisters and

Vivaldi, we would like to include an amazing statement by the Italian musicologist Gabriele Fantoni who, in a book published without date in Milan,[7] flatly asserts that Anna Giraud was Vivaldi's legitimate wife. We can hardly imagine a statement like that, made by (presumably) a Catholic in a Catholic country, to be pure invention. But we shall soon see that Vivaldi's noble colleague, Benedetto Marcello, was to be married in secret, to a beautiful singer ... Perhaps there is some confusion here between the two distinguished Venetians.

We shall soon follow Vivaldi abroad. Obviously the music preceded the man, as the Amsterdam publications found their rapid way all over Europe. One capital where they were received rapturously was Paris, where we have no record that Vivaldi was ever a visitor: but he was involved with France all the same.

The Concert Spirituel in Paris performed Vivaldi's *The Four Seasons* on 7 February 1728, apparently complete, because the *Mercure de France*[8] of February 1728 reports about the concert: 'They played afterwards the Concerto of the four seasons by M. Vivaldi which is an excellent piece of symphony [*sic*] ...'. In the concerts of 4 and 5 April of the same year the soloist was J.P. Guignon, who according to the *Mercure de France* played 'Spring' from *The Four Seasons*, which was repeated on 21 February 1729. On 25 November 1730, at Marly, the King (Louis XV) expressly asked for it: '... Le Roi demanda ensuite qu'on joüat le *Printemps* de *Vivaldi*, qui est une excellent Piece de simphonie', said the writer, repeating his earlier words. He then goes on to add that, 'since the royal musicians do not usually participate in the Marly concerts,' the Prince de Dombes, the Count d'Eu 'and various other *seigneurs* of the court were glad to accompany *le sieur* Guignon so as not to deprive H.M. of the opportunity to hear this fine piece of symphony, which was executed to perfection' (*Mercure de France*, December 1730). Suddenly it was 'Spring' that took Paris by storm, and continued to do so even as late as 1803, when it was 'applaudissait toujours avec transport'.

We now come to Vivaldi's most famous cantata, a song in praise of Paris, which in his eccentric spelling he entitled *La Senna festeggiante* (*The Seine feted*). Michael Talbot, in a particularly brilliant piece of research[9] has convincingly proposed that this Serenata was 'performed, each of its two parts separately, on the occasion of the Public Entry into Venice of the French Ambassador Jacques-Vincent Languet, Count of Gergy (4th and 5th November 1726).' It was not the first time that Vivaldi had been asked to compose a Serenata for Languet, who was appointed in 1721 and served at Venice from 1721 to 1731. At a soirée given on 12 September 1725 to celebrate the wedding of Louis XV and the Polish princess Maria Leszczynska the week before, Vivaldi performed his Serenata *La Gloria* (RV 687) with the appropriate soloists representing La Gloria (contralto) and Imeneo (soprano).[10]

La Senna festeggiante is a Serenata on the very largest scale, really almost the size of a small opera; there is a *sinfonia* with twenty-one numbers in the first part, followed by a French *Ouverture* and fifteen numbers in the second. Unlike the operas of the period, however, there are more accompanied recitatives (ten) than secco recitatives (seven). There are also eleven arias, three duets and three *cori* (three-parts, but by solo voices). The figures are The Seine (*La Senna*), bass; The Golden Age (*L'Età dell'oro*), soprano; and Virtue (*La Virtù*).

For this praise of France and its monarch – the figures wander in search of true happiness and find it on the banks of the Seine – Vivaldi makes a conscious attempt to write in the French style, even to the tempo indication 'Largo alla francese', the frequent use of French dotting (which should be double-dotted in performance, of course) and three-four time. No autograph survives, but the manuscript in Turin has been corrected and annotated by the composer himself. It shows signs of having been radically shortened, and Michael Talbot has persuasively argued that at least one, possibly more, numbers were removed between No. 11, 'Pietà, dolcezza fanno il suo volto' (La Senna) and No. 12, 'Stelle, con vostra pace' (La Virtù). One has the distinct impression that the composer was attempting to write a work of special merit, and took a great deal of pains in so doing.

It is, in short, music of great sophistication, as befits a tribute to the country where that commodity has always been found in supreme abundance. 'In many movements', writes Michael Talbot, 'Vivaldi captures the wistful tenderness at the heart of "le gout français" ' and 'Most striking is the treatment of the "versi sciolti", which are set more often as accompagnatos then as simple recitatives, almost in the style of the French "petit air", while the continuo-accompanied recitatives undergo rhythmic diversification including the use of the triple metre, another Gallic feature. This novel approach exemplifies the ability of the serenata genre ... to accommodate devices unsuited to the more tightly structured and convention-bound domain of baroque opera.'

Vivaldi was conspicuously back at San Angelo and, as we have seen, elsewhere in Venice. The French Ambassador, Jacques-Vincent Languet, again enters our story a year after *La Senna festeggiante*. On 19 September 1727, there was a great *festa* at his palazzo, and the *Mercure de France* (October 1727) tells us that about eight o'clock in the evening, there was 'un très beau concert d'Instrumens qui dura près de deux heures, dont la musique, ainsi que celle du Te Deum étoit du fameux Vivaldi.' Alas, this *Te Deum* appears to be irrevocably lost.

At the theatre, Anna Giraud was the star in *Orlando* of 1727 (Alcina), *Farnace* of 1727 (Tamiri; see above), *Rosilena ed Oronta* of 1728 (Oronta) – all these were by her master – but also as Evandro in *Gli odi delusi dal sangue*, a pasticcio by G.V. Pescetti and Baldasare Galuppi, also in 1728.

We have no idea what salary she was paid but another female singer, Lucrezia Baldini, participated in *Farnace* as Selinda, and fortunately Giazotto discovered her contract with Vivaldi as 'direttore delle opere,'[11] dated 13 October 1726. *Farnace* was the third and last opera of the season at San Angelo, and *la* Baldini was to appear only in it, at a fee of 200 ducats, payable in three instalments, the first before the work went on the stage, the second half-way through its run, and the third and final on the Thursday before Lent. 200 ducats was a tidy sum – double what the Pietà had paid Vivaldi annually in 1704, and even in 1725.

The most extraordinary musical event that took place in Venice in 1728 was certainly not Vivaldi's absence after the second opera from San Angelo but Benedetto Marcello's secret marriage with Rosanna Scalfi, a pretty singer of plebeian origins. Why secret? Because according to the Venetian law of 1567 an aristocrat like Marcello would stand to lose totally his rights to wealth (*diritti di censo*) and patrimony. But Marcello applied officially, on 18 May 1728, for such a secret marriage 'which must never see the light of day without my express order'. And two days later, on 20 May, the *Vicario Generale* registered that the marriage had taken place:

> The N.H. [*nobil huomo* = nobleman] Benedetto Giacomo, son of S. E. [his excellency] Agostino Marcello of the parish of Maddalena, and Signora Rosanna Lorenza, daughter of sig. Stefano Scalfi of the Parish of San Marcuola, have contracted marriage, having given their mutual consent ... before me Mauro Mainardi ..., the banns being dispensed with ...'

As witnesses, there were two Jesuit fathers. Marcello was not only a well-known aristocrat but was celebrated in musical circles for his publication, between 1724 and 1727, of fifty *Psalmi* of David, paraphrased and translated into the vernacular by Gerolamo Ascanio Giustiniani. This secret marriage was indeed an extraordinary feat for Marcello to have managed.[12] That it actually remained a secret must be deduced from a letter that Abbé Conti wrote shortly after all this, on 23 September 1728, in which he states that Marcello had decided to abandon music and his worldly life and devote himself to religion. 'They even say he wants to become a Jesuit or Capucin monk. I am very annoyed about this, because his compositions had a merit above others, not only by their expression of character but also by their strength, or the novelty of their harmonic ideas.' How are we to interpret this document in the light of his marriage to Rosanna Scalfi? There are no documents to help us further.

We now turn from northern Italy to Tuscany, and specifically to the Teatro alla Pergola in Florence, with which Vivaldi was sporadically associated. Recently, a series of no fewer than fifty-two letters addressed from the impresario of that theatre to Vivaldi has come to light, the contents of which we propose to summarize here. They were first discovered by William C. Holmes and published for the first time in 1988 ('Vivaldi e il Teatro La Pergola a Firenze: nuovi fonti' in: *Nuovi Studi Vivaldiani*, ed. Antonio Fanna and Giovanni Morelli, 2 vols., Florence 1988, 1, pp. 117–130).

The impresario was Marchese Luca Casimiro degli Albizzi (1664–1745), who has left us a large file of some 3,000 letters and notes, including the fifty-two to Vivaldi out of a total of 107 in which the composer is mentioned. This correspondence comes from the Albizzi family archives and is now part of the Guicciardini library. As a member of the Accademia degli Immobili alla Pergola, the Marquis was chosen to be the director of the Theatre attached to the Academy, when it reopened on 22 June 1718 with Vivaldi's *Scanderbeg*. The composer was destined to compose three more operas for Florence, *Ipermestra* (Carnival, 1726–7), *L'Atenaide* (Carnival, 1728–9) and *Ginevra principessa di Scozia* (Carnival, 1735–6). The Marquis's correspondence with Vivaldi dates from 1726 to 1739. Unfortunately none of the composer's letters to Albizzi has survived, and there is no correspondence relating to the first opera, *Scanderbeg*, except for a letter of recommendation to Anna Maria Luisa de' Medici, the Palatine Electress, from Mantua dated 30 May 1718.

Vivaldi's second opera for La Pergola was *Ipermestra*, first performed on 25 January 1727, and our correspondence opens with a letter from the Marquis to Vivaldi of 6 July 1726, in which the impresario asks the composer if he would be willing to compose an opera for the coming season. But six days later a similar letter was dispatched to Porpora, who seems to have turned down the proposal, because on 17 August the Marquis repeats his offer to Vivaldi, stipulating the fee as '100 taler which are thirty doubloons of Julius [X, the Pope] at thirty each ['talleri cento che sono double trenta di giuli trento l'uno']. Vivaldi accepted and in a letter of 31 August Albizzi confirms the contract, informing the composer that his will be the second opera of the season and listing the singers of the company. In the correspondence, in which the Marquis says that he has sent the libretto, there is no specific mention of *Ipermestra* by Salvi until a letter to Giovanni Domenico Cottini of Venice; but Albizzi was also considering another text, *Le frenesie d'amore ossia Il savio delirante*, a *burletta* or *opera buffa*, which had been written and composed by Giuseppe Maria Buini, and which was running at S. Moisè in Venice during May and June of that year. But finally the choice fell on *Ipermestra*, and by the end of August the contracts were being drawn up. The correspondence reveals that it was apparently customary for Italian theatres to cooperate with each other, for on 5 October 1726 Albizzi wrote to Michele Grimani of San Giovanni Cristosomo in Venice concerning a production of *Ipermestra* given there by Giacomelli in 1724:

Having observed that at Your Excellency's theatre *Ipermestra* was given in the year 1724, in which I also saw a stage set representing a scene in moonlight and another with the sun; and if these are of no further use and are perhaps able to be transported, I beg you to inform me what would be the costs and also what was the material used for the lighting and how was it set in motion. Inasmuch as I shall be producing the same opera at The Pergola in Florence, although by a different poet, I could include these sets which are bound to please the public and which are perhaps of no use to Your Excellency. Please forgive this intrusion and I remain, etc.

We have no further documents relating to this affair.

The third opera in which Vivaldi was involved with La Pergola was *L'Atenaide*, libretto by Apostolo Zeno, which opened the Carnival season on 29 December 1728 (usually the opening was on the Feast of St Stephen, 26 December). On this occasion Anna Giraud made her début in Florence in the role of Pulcheria in Vivaldi's opera and as Emilia in the second work of the season, Vinci's *Catone in Utica* (libretto by Metastasio). After the season was over Albizzi was curious as to *la* Giraud's reactions and a friend in Venice answered:

La Girò has never been at my house ... but at third hand I have discovered that she is reported to have been very pleased with all the generosity she was shown [in Florence] ...

Giraud may have been pleased by Florence, but Florence was not pleased by Vivaldi: *L'Atenaide* was a flop. The Florentine Ferdinando Bartolommei writes on 5 January 1729 from Vienna to Albizzi:

I am persuaded that it is becoming increasingly difficult to put on operas in that theatre [La Pergola], as witness the poor reception of L'Atenaide and I hope that the reaction to the other one which you intend to stage will be more encouraging, or at least you will be enabled to repair the damage caused by the first. But at best our country [Tuscany] is not nowadays made for such festivities and *divertimenti*: or perhaps they don't understand or are too limited.

Another correspondent, Camillo Pola in Venice, writes on 22 January 1729, 'I would like your Catone, which you are about to stage, to make up for the losses you suffered with the first opera, and that it succeeds and reaps the praise it has received with Grimani', referring to *Catone in Utica*, then running in the setting of Leonardo Leo at San Giovanni Cristosomo in Venice, where it was not, however, Leo's score that was filling the house but the presence of the great castrato Farinelli, 'since among living singers he is the most important.'

Vinci's *Catone in Utica* was much better received in Florence than Vivaldi's opera, and from Venice Pola writes on 18 February 1729 to Albizzi, 'You will soon be at the end of your troubles and I am pleased that the Catone you put on is a success, and I hope you can cover all the losses you suffered with Atenaide.'

Albizzi was 65 years of age and lived on to a ripe old age. In 1732, at 68, he signed his last contract as impresario for a period of six rather than three years. The old marquis wrote modestly to Count Domenico Schianteschi at Parma: 'The gentlemen of the Academy [of the Immobili] having wished me to continue as impresario for another 6 years, which is ridiculous at my advanced age, I agreed to wait upon them as best I could ...'

Vivaldi's final opera for La Pergola was to be *Ginevra principessa di Scozia*, first performed at Florence on 17 January 1736. The first extant news of the new season in the Albizzi correspondence occurs in a letter of 16 April 1735, when the Impresario writes to Vivaldi:

It was only yesterday that the gentlemen resolved to put on operas during the coming Carnival season. I immediately proposed signora Annina [Giraud] as *prima donna*; oh, what

106

opposition they made, saying that she is not on the same level as those who came here later and which they didn't find when you were here the last time ...

This refers, obviously, to the flop of *L'Atenaide*. As for Vivaldi composing a new opera, Albizzi explains that for some time another composer, Giuseppe Maria Orlandini, had been engaged to bring up to date all the old operas in the Pergola's repertoire. But nevertheless, the Marquis proved to be persuasive and by 18 June 1735 the *scrittura* for Vivaldi could be issued at a fee of sixty ducats Julius X, and Anna Giraud would be invited to appear, too:

It is now established that Signora Annina Girò will appear during the future Carnival season in the via della Pergola; and for Your Gracious Self [*Vostra Signoria*] to compose an opera which will certainly be the last of the season [the most prestigious] and not the first as Your Gracious Self feared, I think Ginevra of Doctor Salvi, a very fine libretto which will do honour to everyone. It is no longer a question of the above-named young lady, whom I have supported in contrast to those who have written against her.

By 1 July 1735 the Marquis is calling Vivaldi 'caro signor Antonio' and not 'Vostra Signoria', and as for *la* Girò, Albizzi explains politely and for the last time that

when they were in Venice last Ascension Day, they told me that [Anna Giraud] was a good actress but you couldn't hear her voice ... Let us cease all this, saying that I had to support her when I established that she would sing at Carnival time and let us speak no more about it.

The other opera for the coming season in which *la* Girò was to sing was *Cesare in Egitto* by Bussani and Giacomelli, which would open the *stagione* and in which Anna would sing Cornelia. Otherwise, Albizzi could not send the libretto of *Ginevra* because the Pergola's house poet, Damiano Marchi, had not yet 'put it in order.'

Meanwhile, however, Vivaldi had decided that Salvi's *Ginevra* was not a good vehicle for Anna Giraud and suggested instead Zeno's *Merope*; to which the Marquis replied on 9 July 1735, returning to 'Vostra Signoria' as a more formal address:

> Your Gracious Self tells me in yours of the 2nd that instead of Ginevra we should do Merope because Signora Annina would appear to better advantage. This libretto has been done and re-done in Florence, and there isn't anybody who doesn't remember it. La Ginevra of Pratolino [1708] has not been done since, and I must vary my libretti as much as possible, this being a demanding theatre.

Eventually all was resolved in favour of *Ginevra*, and on 6 August Albizzi sent the revised libretto to Vivaldi, adding 'Your Gracious Self has all the convenience and time to do honour to the composition, for in general it is the final opera [of any given season] which commands the most attention.' Later he cautions Vivaldi not to send the score until it is completed. The composer continued to be contentious, and finally, on 20 August, Albizzi lost his patience:

> Concerning the first paragraph of Your Gracious Self's letter of 16 August, that you are most unwilling to compose the opera because of the limited ability of the musicians in my company, if you are really in such a low state please consider that I shall be glad to absolve you of your obligation. Return the libretto, which I shall cause to be composed by another.

This problem having been settled rapidly, Vivaldi then decided to lay his hands on the other opera, *Cesare in Egitto*, with which he had nothing whatever to do, in order to make it more suitable for Anna Giraud; to which Albizzi replied on 17 September 1735 as follows:

> You can not touch the book of Cesare in Egitto, of which the parts are already copied, and I shall soon be sending that of signora Annina. I agreed to let you modify many of the words in the arias of Ginevra, but as for those removed and altered by our poet signor Marchi, I don't want to offend him, and I must tell you that

the Tuscans have this vanity, not to be considered second to any in matters of poetry. And I must ask you not to be precipitate with Ginevra, much as it is expected in Florence. If you want to remove 'il dado è tratto' or 'o duce il piacerti' or 'duce il vederti', go ahead and do so, but you are not to touch the substance of the libretto nor the division of the acts, because that is the way I wish it. I know you say it is all to improve it, but in Florence I know what is needed.

It was similar in the case of the old arias, dusted off by their composer and re-introduced into a new opera. On 23 September 1735, Albizzi writes to Vivaldi:

When you shall have received the order to compose the opera Ginevra, which you will consign to signore Cottini, you will do as I said and said repeatedly to you, not to seek out [from earlier operas] old arias and then include them arbitrarily as you see fit. And if in the theatre they recognize them, you know that such a thing does no credit to you, and perhaps those who sing the parts are obliged to change them anyway, and that means the loss comes out of my pocket.

Albizzi was a clever diplomat, and when one of the performers, the tenor Pietro Baranti wrote, suggesting some changes in the part to be sung by his daughter (who was also part of the troupe), the impresario answered:

I don't disapprove of the idea that Your Gracious Self proposes in your letter of the 16th to change the aria [in *Cesare in Egitto*] on behalf of your daughter. I permit this because it is not a new score. But in that of Vivaldi you must sing everything he sends.

On 12 November 1735, Albizzi received the complete score from Vivaldi and writes:

I have received the score of Ginevra and in excellent condition ... I have read your list of considerations. I shall put them into practice and especially that which concerns signor Tanfani, the leader of the violins. I don't object to the few words in the recitatives which you have changed, but as for the arias, I think you have taken unwarranted liberties; I have counted twelve, and I abhor totally those which have been composed like this and which block the action when they ought to reprimand, or exhort, or pray. Enough, I shall see that everything shall be done according to your intentions and I shall see to the copyist ... Let me know the costs of transport for the singers' parts and for copying their music, and everything for the paper and binding, for such matters will also be reimbursed.

We have no further notice how the opera was received at Florence. Vivaldi continued to help Albizzi, particularly in the recruiting of ballerinas for La Pergola, for which the composer even on occasion organized the contracts. But in the end Albizzi became disenchanted with the endless intrigues surrounding Vivaldi, particularly in the case of a famous contralto singer, Maria Maddalena Pieri (Albizzi's protegée and, apparently, his mistress as well), whom Vivaldi was supposed to engage as *prima donna* for the 1736 season at Modena. As a result, the Marquis advised Pieri not to accept a whole series of other offers, including Palermo, Milan and Lisbon. On 19 November 1736, Albizzi writes to Vivaldi that

> having trusted in your assertions, I agreed to take la signora Girò as *prima donna* and to ask you to compose the opera; [but the result was that Pieri,] on account of these procedures, is at home without work ... You understand perfectly well what I want to say with all these exaggerations: I can be duped once, but not twice.

One can not escape the impression that Vivaldi was sailing his vessel perilously close to the wind.

IX
Vivaldi and the Emperor Charles VI

꙳

Vivaldi states in the letter of which we have quoted a part above, that he was called to Vienna. This trip must be connected with the dedication of his new compositions, Opus IX *La Cetra* (twelve concertos), issued by Le Cène after 31 January 1727 (when their imminent publication was announced in the *Gazette d'Amsterdam*), to the Emperor Charles VI, one of the many highly musical Habsburgs. We do know that the next year, Vivaldi was generously received by the Emperor at Trieste. In a letter of 19 September 1728, Abbé Conti writes to Madame de Caylus (having previously explained that 'The Emperor made his entry into Gorizia clad like a Spaniard ... The Emperor remained two days at Trieste but he didn't go either to Bucari or to Fiume ...'): 'The Emperor gave a lot of money to Vivaldi, with a chain and a gold medal; and tell him [the son of Madame Caylus] that he ennobled him ...'. Four days later we read: '... The Emperor is not too happy with his Trieste ... [He] had a long talk with Vivaldi about music, they say that in fifteen days he spoke to him more than to his ministers in two years.... His taste for music is very developed ...'.[1] Vivaldi, perhaps during his Viennese or Trieste sojourns, presented Charles VI with a new set of violin concertos, also entitled *La Cetra* and dated 1728 on the autograph parts, which are now preserved in the Österreichische Nationalbibliothek, and which are not at all identical with the published *La Cetra* of Opus 9.[2] Another work apparently composed for the Austrian Emperor is a lost Serenata 'Le gare della Giustizia e della Pace' (RV 689), listed in a 'Catalogo delle compositioni musicali. Continiente, oratori sacri, componimenti da camera, senerate, et opere. Composte, e rappresentate, sotto il gloriosissimo governo della Sacra Cesarea e Real Cattolica Maestà di Carlo VI'.[3]

The title of the second, MS. set of *La Cetra* in Vienna is: 'La Cetra / Concerti / Consecrati / alla Sacra Cesarea Cattolica Real Maestà / Di Carlo VI / Imperatore / L'anno 1728'.

Whether Vivaldi was in Austria in 1728 can not now be determined, but it seems very clear from documentary evidence that he went to Bohemia in 1729 or 1730. On 30 September 1729, Giovanni Battista Vivaldi, his father, petitioned the procurators of S. Marco, where he was still, in his seventies, engaged as violinist, for permission to leave Venice for a year 'to accompany a son to Germany.' The average Italian's idea of Germany included, of course, Austria and thus also Bohemia, which then was a part of the Austrian monarchy. In the event Giovanni Battista's name subsequently disappears from the records of Saint Mark's, and his substitute, one Francesco Negri, retained Vivaldi's position for more than twenty years; so it is presumed that he died on his long tour, which probably took more than just the one year for which permission was asked.[4]

Recently, a series of four letters to a German nobleman, whose name has not been hitherto attached to that of Vivaldi, has come to light. Since the final letter is dated June 1730, it seems opportune to insert this correspondence here.

The new figure on the Vivaldian stage is Carl Ludwig Friedrich, born in 1708, the younger half-brother of Adolph Friedrich III, Duke of Mecklenburg-Strelitz; both were sons of the dynasty's founder, Adolph Friedrich II. On 7 August 1728 Duke Carl left the ducal castle Mirow and started on a 'grand tour' accompanied by a major domo (*Hofmeister*), a councillor, a page, a *valet-de-chambre* and several lackeys. The trip took the party first to Geneva, where they remained until the autumn of 1728, the Duke having completed his studies there to the satisfaction of all. The group then proceeded to Turin, Milan and Parma, and from there to Venice, where Carl and his entourage arrived on Christmas Eve 1728. In a letter to Mirow Castle dated 15 January 1729, Carl reports of his happy sojourn, noting that 'this year the opera is very fine, inasmuch as all the most famous singers such as Faustina, Senesino, Farinello [*sic*], etc. are here ... I have meanwhile started to study music with the famous Vivaldi.'

The young man, just turned twenty-one, was a flautist. He seems, according to the first three letters, to have participated in all sorts of music-making with the composer, including rehearsals. All this took place in January 1729, and on the 29th of that month, Duke Carl writes that he will leave 'next Monday' (31 January) for Bologna, Ferrara and Rome. After spending Carnival and Easter in Rome, the young nobleman continued his travels, arriving at the end of the year in Vienna, where he was received at court in December 1729. As the contents of the fourth Vivaldi letter indicate, the composer seems to have met his noble pupil once again, probably in April 1730, perhaps in connection with the composer's trip to Prague. It is probable that they met in Vienna, where the Duke was now part of the Imperial and Royal Austrian army.[5]

I

Most Serene Highness
I have the honour to present my most humble respects to Y.S.H. and to send the music in question. At the same time I inform Y.S.H. that if it be convenient you send your page to my house at <u>24</u> o'clock* with the two second flute parts for The Concerti à 3, tomorrow morning I will be ready to play them with Y.S.H. Meanwhile I repeat my vivid desire to obey your every command with all marks of respect, [etc.]
    Y.S.H.'s most affectionate, devoted and humble servant
                            Antonio Vivaldi
Undated

II

Most Serene Highness
this evening there will be a rehearsal in S. Casciano, as Y.S.H. has commanded; and I shall go at <u>24</u> [o'clock] to Y.S.H.'s house to accompany you and shall have the honour to wait on you at the rehearsal. And Y.S.H. shall come to be with me this evening and I shall remain at home. Meanwhile with all respects [etc.]
    Y.S.H.'s most affectionate, devoted and humble servant
                            Antonio Vivaldi
Undated

---

* At that time, the setting of the sun marked the end of one day and the beginning of the next; '<u>24</u> o'clock' therefore meant something like 8 p.m., or earlier if it was winter.

III

Most Serene Highness

after the first I now add the second ticket, advising Y.S.H. that this evening at home there will be a rehearsal of Signora Faustina [Hasse] where at <u>24</u> (o'clock) I shall come to fetch Y.H., and I hope that it will please you to come. Meanwhile with all marks of respect, [etc.]

> Y.S.H.'s most affectionate, devoted and humble servant,
> Antonio Vivaldi

IV

Serene Highness

since the honour Y.S.H. favoured me was like a passing shadow, I must search for something else to console me for a longer time and that will be the written intercourse with Y.S.H.

Thanks be to God, I arrived in good health in Venice, where I want to stay in the future. Therefore I lack nothing of perfect contentment if only Y.S.H. would find me worthy of even the smallest task I could do for Y.H. to console me in my fate to be so far away from you that I can not serve you in person.

My most kind Lord, I implore you never to deprive me of your Protection and to believe me that I shall never forget a Prince who has so many qualities and merits. I would like to know if you still find pleasure in playing the flute and if your page behaves well. I beg the innate goodness of Y.S.H. to convey my respects to your major domo and to believe in my most devoted veneration and respect for Y.S.H., [etc.]

> I remain your most affectionate, devoted and humble servant
> Antonio Vivaldi

Venice, 10 June 1730

In February 1730, the Venetian theatre San Giovanni Crisostomo staged a new work by Johann Adolph Hasse entitled *Artaserse*, the libretto by Metastasio, with a cast of star singers. It was the Venetian début of Hasse and the beginning of his meteoric career in Italy, together with his wife Faustina Bordoni. Vivaldi's operatic style was obviously becoming old-fashioned; people preferred the

Hasse team. For the Hasse opera, the cast included Castore Antonio Castori (fee: 4,400 lire), Francesca Cuzzoni, of Handelian fame (22,000 lire), the brilliant castrato Farinelli (Carlo Broschi, 18,600 lire), Nicolini, also of Handelian fame (Niccolò Grimaldi, 12,400 lire), while Metastasio reaped 3,300 lire, apparently having been paid twice for the same 'original' libretto in two places, the second being in Naples with music by Vinci. It is instructive to compare these fantastic fees with that of Vivaldi when, as impresario (and secondly as composer) of the Verona season 1735, he earned 700 ducats (one ducat, or *ducato corrente* = 6 lire and 4 soldi, i.e. some 4,200-odd lire).[6]

Anna Giraud made her final appearance – at least for some years – at San Angelo in Johann Adolph Hasse's opera *Dalisa*, given on Ascension Day 1730. Thereupon, presumably, she, Vivaldi, Vivaldi's father and possibly Paolina set off for Prague, where an Italian opera troupe from Venice, under Antonio Denzio, was having a great success playing Italian operas in the theatre of Franz Anton, Count von Spork. He had arrived there in 1724 and remained in the Bohemian capital for a decade.

Vivaldi took with him his successful *Farnace*, which he caused to be staged at Prague in 1730, to be followed by a new work, *Argippo*, that same autumn. Michael Talbot has located trios dedicated to Count Wrtby, probably Johann Joseph, who was royal governor, president of the Court of Appeal and hereditary treasurer. He seems to have attended *Farnace*, for his copy of the libretto notes that it was received with 'great approbation', while that of *Argippo* is marked 'with very great approbation'.[7] And Vivaldi's church music began to circulate in Bohemia at that time, too: in 1959 I found a contemporary copy of the *Magnificat* in the former library of Osek Monastery (now in the National Museum, Prague), which I edited for Universal Edition as *Magnificat Ossecensis*.

It is not possible to say when Vivaldi returned to Italy. It has been suggested that he would not have wanted to miss his own opera, *La fida Ninfa*, given at Verona to inaugurate the new Teatro Filarmonico on 6 January 1732. (Vivaldi, incidentally, was not Verona's first choice of composer: just as Prague in 1791 would have preferred Antonio Salieri to Mozart, so Verona would have preferred G.M. Orlandini to Vivaldi).[8] It is also not known if he supervised the production of his *Semiramide* at Mantua in 1732, in which year they also revived *Farnace* there (it was also given in 1731 at Pavia), or the revival of *Doriclea* at Prague, followed there by *Dorilla in Tempe*.

Lacking a proper daily newspaper at Venice, as existed in London, our knowledge of many public events must come from diaries and letters. One such letter, preserved in the family archives of the addressee, is from January 1732 from Pier Caterino Zeno, brother of the famous librettist Apostolo Zeno, to Count Daniele Florio in Udine,[9] in which we learn of a 'most splendid *funzione*'. A sacred relic of Saint Pietro Orseolo was brought in procession to the Basilica of St Mark's:

Two monks from Cassano arrived with the most precious relic and were lodged in the monastery of S. Giorgio Maggiore, [where it was venerated by a great number of the faithful. On 7 January] three of the state barges were sent to S. Giorgio; in two of them placed most of the monks of S. Giorgio, with the Cross and silver candles; while in the third which was the finest of the three, the two monks from Cassano were placed, wearing richly embroidered copes. In this barge there was an altar on which was placed the box with the relics. In Riva, waiting, was the clergy of St. Mark's, with flaming torches, and accompanied by musicians who intoned a Laudate Dominum, the most solemn composition of Abbé Vivaldi of the Pietà ... In procession, the relics were carried by one of the two monks into the church of St. Mark's and deposited in the treasury. On the 14th inst. in the presence of the Doge and the whole college, there was celebrated a solemn Mass accompanied by the musicians of the Capella and the relics of the Saint were placed in the middle of the altar, enclosed in a magnificent reliquary. Afterwards there was a procession in which took part the colleagues of all the schools richly dressed, and all the clerical body, the monks, the seminarists and all the rejoicing population ...

It seems, then, that the ecclesiastical authorities were well aware of the value of the church music being composed by the Sig. abbate Vivaldi della Pietà. This was, in all probability, an occasion for which his 'Laudate Dominum' in D minor (RV 606) – the setting of

Psalm 116 – was performed. The Psalm (it is 117 in the King James Bible) for the occasion is 'O Praise the Lord, all ye nations; praise him, all ye people. For his merciful kindness is great towards us: and the truth of the Lord endureth for ever. Praise ye the Lord.'

Our next firm date for Vivaldi in Venice comes from a recently discovered letter dated Venice, 13 February 1733, from Edward Holdsworth to his and Handel's friend and patron Charles Jennens, who had requested Holdsworth to visit Vivaldi and purchase some compositions from him. The letter is full of chatty remarks, for instance about Jennens's harpsichord:

> ... I hope you have by this time found out M.ʳ Bertie's tuner to put yʳ Harpsichord in order. I have wrote to Florence to acquaint the maker wᵗʰ the ill state you found it in on its' arrival, and to complain of his sending it out of his hands in so bad a condition. I suppose he will deny it; and indeed I was very much surpris'd to hear your account of it, because M.ʳ Mequell had it tried by a good master a few days before 'twas sent off, and the maker pack'd it up himself.
>
> I had this day some discourse with your friend Vivaldi, who told me t[ha]t He had resolv'd not to publish any more Concertos, because He says it prevents his selling his Compositions in MSS wᶜʰ He thinks will turn more to account; as certainly it would if He finds a good market, for he expects a Guinea for ev'ry piece. Perhaps you might deal with him if you were here to choose what you like, but I am sure I shall not venture to choose for you at that price. I had before been inform'd by others that this was Vivaldi's reputation. I suppose you already know t[ha]t he has publish'd 17 Concertos ...'[10]

On 2 June 1732 a new Doge was elected in Venice: Carlo Ruzzini, who had proved to be an able diplomat. Under his guidance, writes Giazotto[11] 'the state finances went from bad to worse. It was Ruzzini who insisted on turning Venice into a free port, in competition with those of Trieste and Ancona. This plan was realized in 1736, and one would have expected, with this commercially viable operation, that the financial situation would have improved; but it turned out to be a fictitious improvement: the Body Politic was ill from within'.

One of the towns with which Vivaldi was in contact was Verona, for which he was impresario in 1732 (*La fida Ninfa*) and 1735 (*Adelaide* and *Tamerlano*), and where he would have a great success with *Catone in Utica* in 1737, produced as a single work, i.e. as composer rather than impresario for the whole season. The season of 1735 was complicated by the Polish war of succession, with which reality Vivaldi was confronted when he returned from Bohemia.

Recently, archive material from the Pepoli family in Bologna has been discovered, with autograph correspondence between Vivaldi and the Bolognese nobleman, Count Sicinio Ignazio Pepoli, the second son of Count Cornelio, Bolognese Senator and Maria Caterina Bentivoglio. Sicinio married Eleonora, daughter of Marcantonio Prince Colonna and Diana Paleotti on 8 July 1720. He lived in Bologna in the Palazzo Pepoli-Campogrande, famous for its frescoes by Giuseppe Maria Crespi. Count Sicinio was a keen lover of opera and became patron of the Bolognese noble theatre as well as exercising some artistic control over the new Verona theatre, Il Teatro Filarmonico. The opera *La fida Ninfa* for Verona in 1732 saw the light of day with some difficulty. The castrato Francesco Bilanzoni, singing in Naples in 1731, although offered one hundred zecchini 'in a box' and lavish hospitality, refused; and the 'operetta', as it is referred to in the sources, was hastily mounted, causing one contemporary to say 'not all the singers were very noteworthy, even if it be conceded that it [the opera] was backed in a tardy and limited fashion'.

Now, in 1734, Vivaldi was to mount a new season for the coming year in which the Veronese Count Rambaldo Rambaldi (1693 or 1694–1775) played a notable role. As a member of the famous Veronese Accademia Filarmonica, he also had a notable say in the Verona theatre. In wanting to engage singers, he used as a go-between Count Pepoli.

Vivaldi's position was probably compromised seriously by a curious episode involving Anna Giraud, her 'protector' Piero Pasqualigo and Count Pepoli's elder brother Alessandro. They may have admired Vivaldi as a musician but the whole Pepoli entourage seems to have taken a very jaundiced view of Vivaldi the man. In a letter from Verona of 7 October 1734 to Count Sicinio, Rambaldi writes:

I tried to get Sig^r Pietro Morigi to sing in our theatre for Sig^r Vivaldi, Impresario. These two, after having suggested high terms, have been reduced to writing that they will accept everything I had proposed to them. I offered them a *scrittura* [global fee] of 600 ducats, he returned this proposal, writing that he couldn't do it for less than 800 ducats. Therefore I send to Y.E. a contract with the fee left open and in which I ask you to act as arbiter; hence I beg you to arrange it between 600 and 800 as you see fit, but even if they will not budge from the 800 we must accept it. I beg of you to sign the contract and to send a signed copy direct to me at Venice, whence I shall leave tomorrow ...'

Meanwhile Vivaldi went to Verona, from where he sent the following legal document to Pepoli:

Verona, 7 October 1734.
With the present private contract, which has the same validity as if drawn up by a registered notary public in this city, I, D. Ant:^{o} Vivaldi, who have signed below in my name and in that of the subscribers of the Theatre at Verona, engage S:^{r} Pietro Morighi to sing in all the operas which are to be given in the above-named theatre during the coming Carnival, and in which he declares to attend all the rehearsals and performances. For which I Vivaldi agree in my name and in that of the subscribers to the following honorarium for the afore-said S:^{r} Morighi, viz ducats at the rate of £6:4—— (blank), in words ——. S:^{r} Morighi agrees to pay at his expense the trips, the meals and the lodgings for the entire time that is spent in Verona. *In fede* etc. I, Antonio Vivaldi in my name, and in that of the subscribers, affirm the above ——. [In the hand of Count Rambaldi:] I, Rambaldo Rambaldi, agree to the conditions for the afore-said Sig:^{r} Vivaldi, promising that they will be paid punctually.

The correspondence continues with another autograph letter by Vivaldi to Count Pepoli:

Excellency,
I permit myself to make the following observation to Y.E. on bended knee, that I have the honour to notify you that Count

Rambaldi had arranged to come to Venice when an affair of such importance occurred [the Count was required to wait on the commander of the Imperial armies, Count Lothar Joseph Dominik von Königsegg und Rothenfels, 1673–1751] that after having sent the letters to Bologna he was obliged to remain in Verona. I have undertaken to that gentleman [Count Rambaldi] to forward all letters which arrive here from Bologna for him, this evening I shall not fail speedily to forward that from Y.E. and another from S:ʳ Morighi. Since the above mentioned S:ʳ Count has left everything for the final decision regarding the engagement of said castrato for the two operas which are to be given in Verona, I am persuaded that unbeknown to me every difficulty will be easily resolved in the new answers which Y.E. will receive. Meanwhile I beseech the great generosity of Y.E. to have the goodness to keep your word with the above-mentioned castrato, especially since our theatre of S. Angielo [*sic*], with which he was negotiating, has last week engaged Castor Castorino. I ask a thousand pardons to Y.E. for the bother of having to disturb you with these rude pretensions of mine, which I beg you to attribute to the necessity for acting in this fashion. May Providence find a way to clear the road in this affair, for which I would wish to add myself to the innumerable number of your servants in awaiting the possibility for executing punctually the most honoured sign given by Y.E., that in the future I may have the glory to subscribe myself, with the most fervid veneration, Y.E.'s most humble and obedient servant,

Antonio Vivaldi

Venice, 16 October 1734

The series continues with a short note by Rambaldo Rambaldi, asking Pepoli to sign the contract at his earliest convenience (Verona, 21 October 1734). Two copies were sent, one to be signed by Morigi (wrongly called Morighi) and to be returned to Vivaldi, and the other to be filed 'as a precaution'. His fee was 700 ducats, exactly half of the sum he had originally demanded.

There are two further documents, the first a letter by Vivaldi:

Excellency,

I should once again be in the most favoured grace of Y.E. if you would deign to send to me the contract of S:ʳ Morighi. I had in all humility hoped to receive with it the exceptional honour of a sign from Y.E. in order the more easily to pluck up the courage to wait most humbly on you. Should Y.E. find me worthy, I should accept it with the most profound veneration and shall find all the means to remain, in humility,

Y.E.'s most humble, devoted and obedient servant

Antonio Vivaldi

Venice, 30 October 1734

And here is Vivaldi's petition to the Academy at Verona:

Most illustrious Accademia Filarmonica

With the present [letter] I seek from the illustrious members the permission to use your famous theatre, promising that nothing shall prejudice the performances, on the contrary, that all shall be harmonious, for I have given much thought to the choice of the subjects and for the scenery, and so I dare to hope for the welcome of Your Illustrious Selves and of the whole community, whose approbation I trust that my efforts will merit. With thanks, etc.

Your most humble, devoted and obedient servant

Antonio Vivaldi[12]

It is to be presumed that almost all *stagioni* in Italy and elsewhere had difficult births, but from perusing the documents one can not escape the feeling that for Vivaldi and his entourage of the Giraud sisters, etc., time was beginning to run out. The author of the article on which this section is based is in the process of ordering the Pepoli archives in Bologna, and there is presumably more information to come from that hitherto untapped source.[13]

X
Goldoni and Vivaldi

৵

The famous man of letters, whose statue in Venice greets hordes of daily tourists, now enters Vivaldi's life. In 1735 Carlo Goldoni (1707–93) was a promising young playwright, engaged by Michele Grimani, the owner of the Teatro S. Samuele, to adapt *Griselda* by Apostolo Zeno, which Vivaldi was to compose for the forthcoming Ascension season. Some years before, in 1728, Tommaso Albinoni had composed it, and obviously Vivaldi needed someone to adapt it to his requirements. Twenty-seven years later, in 1761, in the publication of volume XIII of his *Commedie*, Goldoni wrote about this event and made it one of the more amusing stories of his professional life. We reproduce it here in the deft translation of Alan Kendall.[1]

That year, for the Ascension opera, the composer was the priest Vivaldi, known as the red priest because of his hair, and sometimes referred to as Rossi, so that people thought that was his surname.

This most famous violinist, this man famous for his sonatas, especially for those known as the Four Seasons, also composed operas; and although the really knowledgeable people say that he was weak on counterpoint and that he handled his basses badly, he made the parts sound well, and most of the time his operas were successful.

That year the role of the prima donna was to be taken by Signora Annina Girò, or Giraud, the daughter of a wigmaker of French origin, who was commonly called Annina of the red priest, because she was Vivaldi's pupil. She did not have a beautiful voice, nor was she a great musician, but she was pretty and attractive; she acted well (a rare thing in those days) and had protectors: one needs nothing more to deserve the role of prima donna. Vivaldi was very concerned to find a poet who would arrange, or disarrange, the play to his taste, by adapting, more or less, several arias that his pupil had sung on other occasions; since I was the person to whom this task fell, I introduced myself to the composer on the orders of the *cavaliere padrone* [Grimani]. He received me quite coldly. He took me for a beginner and he was quite right; and not finding me very well up in the business of mutilating plays, one could see that he very much wanted to send me packing.

Goldoni's *Il Belisario* had been first performed at S. Samuele on 24 November 1734, and had proved to be a great success. This play was followed in January 1735 by Goldoni's *Rosimonda*, also a success. *Il Belisario* was revived and played to full houses all through Carnival. Goldoni was the rising theatrical star in Venice.

He [Vivaldi] knew the success my *Belisario* had had, he knew how successful my *intermezzi* had been; but the adaptation of a play was something that he regarded as difficult, and which required a special talent, according to him. I then remembered those rules that had driven me mad in Milan when my *Amalasunta* was read, and I too wanted to leave; but my situation and the fear of making a bad impression on His Excellency Grimani, as well as the hope of being given the direction of the magnificent theatre of S. Giovanni Grisostomo [*sic*], induced me to feign and almost to ask the red priest to try me out. He looked at me with a compassionate smile and took up a little book:

'Here,' he said, 'is the play that has to be adapted, Apostolo Zeno's *Griselda*. The work is very fine. The part for the prima donna could not be better. But certain changes are necessary . . . If Your Lordship knew the rules . . . Useless. You cannot know them. Here, for example, after this tender scene, there is a cantabile aria. But since Signora Anna does not . . . does not . . . like this sort of aria (in other words she was incapable of singing it), one needs here an action aria . . . that reveals passion, but not pathos, and is not cantabile.'

'I understand', I replied. 'I will endeavour to satisfy you. Give me the libretto'.

'But I need it for myself', replied Vivaldi. 'When will you return it?'

'Immediately', I replied. 'Give me a sheet of paper and a pen . . .'

'What! Your Lordship imagines that an opera aria is like an intermezzo aria!'

I was furious, and replied to him insolently. He gave me the pen and took a letter from his pocket, from which he tore a sheet of white paper.

'Don't get angry', he said modestly. 'Here sit down at this table. Here is the paper, the pen and the libretto. Make yourself comfortable.'

Then he went back to his worktable and began to say his breviary. I then read the scene carefully. I analysed the sentiment of the cantabile aria and turned it into another of action, passion and motion. I took my work to him. With his breviary in his right hand and my sheet of paper in his left he began to read gently. When he had finished he threw the breviary into a corner, got up, embraced me, ran to the door and called Signora Annina. Annina arrived, with her sister Paolina. He read them the arietta, shouting: 'He did it here, he did it here, on this very spot!' Again he embraced me and congratulated me, and now I had become his friend, his poet, his *confident*, and he never abandoned me. I then murdered Zeno's play exactly as he wanted. The opera was put on successfully. As for me, as soon as the Ascension opera season was over, I took myself off to Padua, where Imer and his company were, to finish off the spring season that year in a mediocre way.

This passage is, of course, immensely valuable to us as a wickedly clever sketch of the 'red priest' at work. It also establishes the two Giraud sisters as a regular part of the Vivaldian entourage. And now comes a curious epilogue. Twenty-six years after Goldoni first issued it, in 1761, he wrote a new version which was published in Paris in French (*Nouveaux mémoires sur l'Italie*, 1787). This second version differs in many important details from the first. The fact that, even though the original account was published and known to the theatrical and literary world, Goldoni insolently offers another and quite different account raises fundamental doubts in any serious biographer's mind. One has always mistrusted these accounts of verbatim conversations, written down decades after they occurred: two particularly well-known 'transcriptions' years after the event are Dittersdorf's famous conversation with Emperor Joseph II on the subject of Haydn and Mozart[2] and Da Ponte's account of collaboration with Mozart, including many long verbatim conversations with Count Orsini-Rosenberg and Emperor Joseph II, published some forty-five years afterwards. (I have shown that Joseph II's remarks about *Don Giovanni* are wholly Da Ponte's invention because we have archival documents showing that Joseph never saw *Don Giovanni*.) Bearing this in mind, we proceed to the second version of the encounter Goldoni–Vivaldi, published more than half a century after the event.[3]

Griselda had been chosen, an opera by Apostolo Zeno and Pariati, who worked together before Zeno left for Vienna in the service of the Emperor, and the composer who was to put it to music was the abbé Vivaldi, who is called, because of his hair, *il Prete Rosso* (the Red Priest). He was better known by this nickname than by his family name.

That clergyman, an excellent violin player and a middling composer, had taught Mlle [Anna] Giraud and given her training in singing; she was a young singer born in Venice, the daughter, however, of a French wigmaker. She was not pretty, but she had charms – a delicate figure, beautiful eyes, beautiful hair, a charming mouth, and not much of a voice but much acting ability. It was she who was to portray the role of Griselda.

M. Grimani sent me to the musician's home in order to make the necessary changes in the opera, be they to shorten the drama or to change the position and the nature of the arias to suit the wishes of the actors and the composer. Therefore, I went to the home of the abbé Vivaldi, I presented myself on behalf of His Excellency Grimani, I found him surrounded by music and with his breviary in hand. He got up, he made a complete sign of the cross, he put his breviary aside, and made me the usual compliments. 'What is the cause of my having the pleasure of seeing you, Monsieur?'

'His Excellency Grimani has entrusted me with the alterations that you think necessary in the opera of the Carnival. I have come to see, Monsieur, what your intentions are.'

'Ah! Ah! Are you entrusted Monsieur, with the alterations in my opera *Griselda*? Then M. Lalli is no longer connected with M. Grimani's productions?'

'M. Lalli, who is very elderly, will always profit from the dedicatory letters and the sales of the librettos, which does not concern me. I have the pleasure of busying myself in work that ought to amuse me, and I have the honour of beginning under the commands of M. Vivaldi.' The abbé took up his breviary again, made another sign of the cross, and did not answer.

'Monsieur', I said to him, 'I do not wish to distract you in your religious pursuit; I shall come back at another time.'

'I am well aware, my dear sir, that you have a talent for poetry; I have seen your *Belisario*, which gave me great pleasure. But this is very different. One may be able to create a tragedy or an epic poem, if you please, and not be able to fashion a musical quatrain.'

'Do me the honour of showing me your drama.'

'Yes, yes, I am willing. Where then is *Griselda* tucked away? It was here ... *Deus in adjutorium meum intende* ... *Domine* ... *Domine* ... *Domine* ... It was here just now. *Domine ad adjuvandum* ... Ah! Here it is. See, Monsieur, this scene between Gualtiero and Griselda; it is an interesting and moving scene. The author has put a pathetic aria at the end, but Mlle. Giraud does not like the languid style of singing. She would like a piece with expression and excitement, an aria that expresses emotion by different means, by interrupted words, for example, by heaved sighs, by action and agitation; I don't know if you understand me.'

'Yes, Monsieur, I quite clearly understand you. Moreover, I have had the honour of hearing Mlle Giraud and I know that her voice is not very strong.'

'Why, Monsieur, do you insult my pupil? She is good at everything; she sings everything.'

'Yes, Monsieur, you are right. Give me the book and allow me to do it.'

'No, Monsieur, I cannot give it up, I need it, and I am very hard pressed.'

'Very well, Monsieur, if you are in a hurry, give me a moment and I shall gratify you at once.'   .

'At once?'

'Yes, Monsieur, at once.'

The abbé, while scoffing at me, held out the drama to me and gave me paper and a writing desk, again took up his breviary and recited his psalms and hymns while walking about. I re-read the scene, with which I was already acquainted. I made a summing up of what the musician wanted, and in less than a quarter of an hour I wrote down the text for an aria of eight lines divided into two parts. I called the clergyman and showed him my work. Vivaldi read it and smoothed the wrinkles from his brow; he read it again and uttered cries of joy; he threw his prayer book on the ground and summoned Mlle Giraud. She came.

'Ah!' he said to her, 'Here is an unusual man, he is an excellent poet. Read this aria. It is this gentleman who has done it here without hedging and in less than a quarter of an hour.' And coming back to me, he said 'Ah! Monsieur, I beg your pardon'. And he embraced me and swore that he would never have another poet but me.

He entrusted me with the drama and ordered the alterations from me. He was always satisfied with me, and the opera succeeded excellently.

One notices that Goldoni has now made of Vivaldi, in Kendall's words, a rather irascible and eccentric old priest, absentmindedly reading from his breviary and not answering Goldoni's remarks. And in this later version of events Vivaldi has now become 'an excellent violinist and a middling composer', rather than the famous composer of *The Four Seasons* as he was in 1761.

An amusing epilogue to this meeting is the production, in the autumn of 1735, of *Aristide* at S. Samuele, by two mysterious gentlemen – the composer 'Lotavio Vandini' and the poet 'Grolo Candido', – though why Antonio Vivaldi and Carlo Goldoni should have wished to remain in semi-anonymity as the authors of this heroic-comic opera is difficult to fathom.[4]

In 1735 Vivaldi was in Verona producing two operas for Carnival season. For one of them, *Adelaide,* he went to the trouble of publishing a dedication in the original edition of the libretto to Antonio Grimani, Vice Podestà of Verona. This dedication, unlike most of the others quoted hitherto, is more interesting and personal; it shows Vivaldi had a genuine respect for this member of one of Venice's most famous and revered families.

> Excellency,
> the common custom of great personages – copying our great Lord God by whom they are destined to govern the cities – to look rather at the soul and the heart of the donor in the occasion of their bringing some offerings, encourages me now to present this musical drama as a sign of my most devoted indebtedness to Your Excellency. I hope also that the sublime display of your name on the frontispiece of the drama will gain me all the benevolence of that venerable nobility for whose entertainment I present it. I recall to have heard several times how strong among the people is the memory of His Excellency Signor Giambattista, Your Excellency's father, who held this post before you, and whose magnificence, justice, courtesy and other virtues won the hearts of these citizens. Since I have heard many remarks how in the short time of your reign you have demonstrated that you will in no way deviate from that glorious example, you will make Your High House even more beloved in this city.
>
> It was likewise befitting to dedicate this drama to a Venetian Patrician, then, since its real history – from which the plot was taken – must be displeasing to a good Italian, who unlike many nowadays inimical to this nation must consider the fact that, having expelled the last Italian kings, miserable Italy fell under the yoke of foreigners from which it can not free itself. Only the venerable Venetian republic gives some compensation to that deplorable misfortune, because from the day of its birth until now the Italian liberty is preserved here and may God continue to preserve it over the centuries. May it also please God long to preserve Your House; the unique branch from which you come

has already shown good characteristics which will not diminish it but will lend more brilliance to the glorious deeds of your ancestors.

Lastly I beg you not to refuse me to subscribe myself publicly with the most profound respect as Your Excellency's most humble, devoted and obedient servant,

Antonio Vivaldi

On 5 August 1735, after a long pause, the Pietà confirmed or rather renewed Vivaldi's contract of 1723 (see above, p. 56). He is still expected to supply concertos but their number is no longer specified. The salary, 100 ducats per annum, remains the same. He was to teach the girls also how to perform the works he submits ('doverà il maestro stesso somministrare a queste nostre figlie concerti e composizioni e doverà portarsi colla dovuta frequenza ad instruire le figlie e renderle capaci della maniera di esiguirli ...'). On 6 September 1735 he was paid by the Pietà authorities 45 lire for 'sonate di musica'. He was reinstated as 'maestro de'concerti' but they reminded him that he was now 'senza idea di più partire come aveva praticato negli anni passati' ('without the idea of leaving as he has done in the past years'). He was still on the Pietà books in 1736.[5]

Another commission came from Florence in 1736 for the Teatro alla Pergola – *Ginevra principessa di Scozia* and the next year from the Teatro Filarmonico in Verona – *Catone in Utica* on a famous text by Metastasio. The first performance, on 26 March, was attended by Charles Albert, Elector of Bavaria, his wife and his brother, Ferdinand. Perhaps Vivaldi was there, for we have a dated letter from him in Verona on 13 May.

XI
Troubles in Ferrara

We now come to the only well documented episode in Vivaldi's life: his frustrating and in the end frustrated attempts to produce operas in Ferrara. The two operas which were given there in 1737 were *Demetrio* and *Alessandro nell'Indie,* both to librettos by Metastasio, but with music by J.A. Hasse, arranged ('edited') by Vivaldi. The 'red priest' was in correspondence with Marquis Guido Bentivoglio, and these autograph letters – the only lines by Vivaldi to have survived – and drafts of the Marquis's answers, are uniquely valuable. Part of this correspondence was discovered in the latter part of the nineteenth century in the Archivio di Stato in Ferrara, and since then more has turned up. It is published complete in Italian in various journals, with varying degrees of accuracy, to which Francesco Degrada has recently drawn attention.[1] Since some of the autographs are still in private possession, our knowledge of most of those texts derives from transcriptions which are not entirely accurate.

Guido Bentivoglio, a second son, was destined, as was characteristic of family life in Italy (also in England) in those days, for the church. In Rome, where he pursued his studies, he was sponsored by his uncle, Cardinal Cornelio, and it is thought that he met Vivaldi there and a friendship was formed. When his elder brother died, Guido became head of the family and had to return to Ferrara to take up his new duties, renouncing a possibly promising ecclesiastical career. Like most of the Italian nobility, the members of which sang or played an instrument, Bentivoglio played the mandolin: possibly Vivaldi wrote some pieces for him – several survive in the Turin library – or at any rate sent him some which he had written for other purposes. For the first time in English, therefore, we propose to publish all this correspondence – Vivaldi's, complete and unabridged, the rest in shortened form. Letters are always the most important and revealing sources for a biographer, and we probably learn more about Vivaldi the man from this correspondence than from any other source.

The correspondence begins with a lost letter from Vivaldi to Bentivoglio of 20 October 1736, in which the composer proposes to mount an operatic season at Ferrara in the coming winter. Bentivoglio answers that Abbé Bollani, the Ferrara Opera's impresario, will be in Venice to discuss the matter with Vivaldi. When Vivaldi replies, on 3 November, Abbé Bollani has arrived in Venice and the first negotiations have been successful. Vivaldi at first refuses the third opera of the season at S. Cassiano in Venice, demanding 100 zecchini, his usual fee, instead of the 90 offered. Vivaldi offers two of his operas especially arranged for Ferrara for the price of six zecchini, which is just the copyist's charges. He is unable to go to Ferrara in person because of his work at S. Cassiano, but Anna Girò, who will be part of the Ferrara troupe, presents her compliments.

> Excellency. The infinitely great kindness of Y.E. lets me rest assured that you will never forget your most welcome promises made in Rome and think me always worthy of your esteemed protection. I swear to Y.E. that the appearance of S. Abbate Bollani surprised me as much as it has pleased me. I do not hesitate to thank Y.E. and to minimize the annoyance for you, and also because my poor pen would not suffice to show my dutiful gratitude to you. I really hope that in dealing with the before-mentioned Signor Abbate, Y.E. will know that I have no other design in this enterprise than to demonstrate my humblest esteem and to organize a theatre as it should be. I assert Y.E. that one has formed here such a company which, I trust, will not for years to come have been seen in Carnival time on the stage at Ferrara.
> The greatest part of the artists have performed many times in first-rate theatres and each one has his (or her) special merit. Y.E., on my word of honour, will find himself well served and will

be content even before you hear the company. After I had refused to compose the third opera for San Cassiano for 90 zecchini, they had to give me my usual 100. Therefore Ferrara will have two operas which will seem to be made for them on purpose, because all are adapted and written by me for only six zecchini an opera, which is the salary of a copyist. This is the humble sacrifice I made for the very kind mediation of Y.E. I am very sorry that I can not come personally, because the above mentioned opera of S. Cassiano prevents me. In any case, if it is possible for me I will be at the feet of Y.E. at the end of Carnival. La signora Anna Girò assures Y.E. of her humblest respect and thenceforth you will kindly put up with her imperfections in Ferrara, and she begs also most earnestly that you may grant her your most valid patronage. Full of the favours granted I can do no more than to look out for every little sign of Y.E. to be your etc.

Antonio Vivaldi

Ferrara, 3 November 1736

The next letter deals with the problems of a contract with the singer Rosa Mancini. Vivaldi has been obliged to rewrite the recitatives in Hasse's *Demetrio* and also to compose some new arias. This opera, destined for Ferrara, is in rehearsal in Venice.

Excellency. The honour of being able to serve Y.E. has meant that my entire attention has been turned towards the opera at Ferrara. I hear from Sig. Lanzetti that the impresario is about to make a mistake over the contract with Signora Mancini. He is mistaken in thinking that the contract had been signed for a period of sixteen days, forgetting that it ought to be sent to Venice and not to Ferrara from whence it would come into his hands. I can assure Y.E. that Mancini is a lady singer of such qualities that she improves the image of the company, whereas on the contrary *la* Moscovita and *la* Natalizia are only beginners and hence but capable of singing small roles. Today Sig. Lanzetti sent to the former the role in the first act [of Hasse's opera *Demetrio*, which had been given at S. Giovanni Cristosomo in 1732] and this only as a precautionary measure, whereas everyone would regret that this good company would be weakened. Considering the fact that all the singers' roles in *Demetrio* have to be switched round and that will cause mistakes, I have decided to compose all the recitatives afresh and to provide the singers with a great many of my arias. The first act has gone out [to the copyist] and all the singers will know their parts before they leave Venice. I would much rather know if I shall have the fortune to satisfy Y.E. and I beg you to believe that it will be my greatest fame to seek the means whereby I, together with Madame Girò, may show you our most profound respect. I remain, Y.E.'s most devoted, obedient and humble servant,

Antonio Vivaldi

Venice, 24 November 1736

The composer trusts that *Demetrio* has been a success in Ferrara. Meanwhile he sends the first act of another for the copyist. He includes some changes for Bentivoglio's approval, rather than sending them to the impresario Bollani, who might 'get excited'. The impresarios of S. Cassiano, S. Angelo, Brescia and Ferrara are all found wanting.

Excellency. I do not present myself to Y.E. to follow the ancient custom of many who wish for your well-being only once a year, but I present my humblest compliments and desire for nothing more than that the family of Y.E. will be blessed to the utmost till eternity. I imagine that the opera was performed, and I hope it was done as I would have wished it.

I will send today the first act, revised and ready for the copyist, but since I find it necessary to change a few verses to improve it, I take the liberty of including it herewith so that you may at your ease peruse and examine it with your great knowledge, because if I send it to the Impresario, he would get too excited.

It seems this is the year of the inexperienced impresarios, they are all the same in S. Cassiano, S. Angelo and also in Brescia. I do not talk about the one in Ferrara.

I cannot express enough how much I desire to come to Ferrara just to pay Y.E. my respects. I implore Y.E. to let me know if you still enjoy the mandolin.

I beg Y.E. that your innate kindness allows me your lasting patronage and that I am permitted to subscribe myself to be, with the greatest respect, Y.E.'s your most devoted and obliged servant.

Antonio Vivaldi

Venice, 26 December 1736

Vivaldi had originally agreed with Bollani to perform two operas, *La Ginevra* and *L'Olimpiade*, the former having been composed for Florence in 1736 and the latter in 1734 for Venice. After having completed the revisions of the former, Bollani informed the composer that the Ferrara patrons would prefer Hasse's *Demetrio*. Vivaldi obtained the score from the house of Grimani and proceeded to revise it thoroughly, involving an additional expense of 20 lire. Vivaldi was also busy revising *L'Olimpiade* and having it copied, only to hear from Bollani that instead, Ferrara proposed to stage *Alessandro nell'Indie* (Hasse?). Bollani suggested that Grimani furnish the score. Vivaldi arranges to have the score copied at a further expense of six zecchini, and the composer is therefore owed six zecchini and 20 lire. Vivaldi stresses the incompetence of the whole Ferrara operation.

The noble sentiments which Y.E. condescends to express in your highly appreciated letter makes me believe that you still keep me in your memory. They are nothing else than the reflection of your kindness and an indication of your clemency. I am incapable of explaining why I find such delight while realizing that I cause Y.E. much trouble. Allow me therefore to bring to your attention and your most prudent consideration this little point which has come to my mind without my telling anybody. The revered Ab. Bollani persuaded me forcefully to give him two operas. La Genevra [*La Ginevra*] and L'Olimpiade,[2] and both to be provided with recitatives for his company for the miserable price of 6 zecchini each. As soon as he returned to Ferrara he tormented me to go immediately to work on La Genevra. I adjusted at once the original, had the parts copied, which I sent to Y.E. as a token of my good will, but the parts of *la* Moro and the tenor are still in their hands. As soon as I had done that there

134

arrives another command, that the gentlemen no longer want La Genevra anymore, but Il Demetrio. So I fetch the original from Cà Grimini to have it copied, but I see that of the six parts, five have to be changed, because the recitatives no longer make sense; therefore – Y.E. can see my good heart – I decided to rewrite all the recitatives. I must warn Y.E. that, apart from the 6 zecchini, I agreed with the Sigr. Impresario to adjust completely Il Demetrio, I will have to have the singers and musicians parts copied and will oblige them to learn them by heart; I shall have three rehearsals and that should be sufficient.

Similar pleasures are surely not to be found in the second opera. All that done, I inform you that I have spent for the copying of the vocal and instrumental parts between La Genevra and Il Demetrio 50 lire, and since for one opera alone the cost should be only 30 lire, so I was obliged to write ten letters up to now that Lanzetti pay me the missing 20; he never answers me on that point.

In many letters he torments me to send him L'Olimpiade. I adjust it, even ruining my original in doing so. I let some of the parts be copied under my very eyes without his orders, because I believe it would be in his interest to see the difference between one copyist and another. And there – another command: he does not want L'Olimpiade any longer, but L'Alessandro in Indie.[3] And he asks for it with the ridiculous suggestion that H.E. Michiel Grimani may send him his original to have it copied in Ferrara, something which an ordinary impresario would never do. Since this was a successful original production I swear to Y.E. that forceful language had to be used with S. Pietro [*sic*] Pasqualigo, but with the understanding that it must be immediately copied by the copyist which the above-mentioned impresario knows and which will cost three zecchini: the original was copied, paid; and all the recitatives adjusted and prepared for the copyist. Only on Wednesday can the letters be sent from Venice; and I wanted in any case to send the first act, and to save the postage I sent it at the cost of four lire more, to Signora Girò through S. Bertelli. In the same way I sent Y.E. the second act and Wednesday I will send the third. S. Impresario wanted to have it corrected at Ferrara to save the three zecchini, but I did not allow that. Therefore the above-mentioned impresario owes me 6 zecchini and 20 lire. Can Y.E. imagine that this impresario merits the corrections of four operas instead of two, the redone recitatives, all the services and on top of it, those expenses? With Y.E.'s generosity, he shall have to reimburse me for all this.

This gentleman does not know how to be a proper impresario, and when one should spend money and when to save. If he had established the whole company in my house, he would not have had that tenor and would have saved 150 scudi. But he wanted to stick to Lanzetti who wanted only to please *la* Becchera, and he deceived himself; for l'Isola and his company did not merit that sum of money. As for myself, after Easter I shall form a large theatrical company, but with care. I ask pardon for this lengthy inconvenience and humbly kiss Y.E.'s hands.

Your most devoted and humble servant
Antonio Vivaldi

Venice, 29 Xbre (December) 1736

In Bentivoglio's reply to this letter, 30 December 1736, the Marquis, not having received the above letter, approves the changes in *Alessandro* and agrees that Bollani is not clever. He admits that he plays his mandolin only about once a year, or less. In his next letter, Vivaldi sends the final act of *Alessandro nell'Indie* to Ferrara. Vivaldi hopes that Bentivoglio will help in paying Bollani's debts. It is said that *Demetrio*, lasting four hours, is too long, but Vivaldi's attempts to shorten the recitatives were prevented by Bollani's assistant Lanzetti.

Excellency. Doing my duty, I send S. Bertelli that he may deliver into the hand of Y.E. the third act, hoping that you have already received the second last Saturday. I invoke the kindness of Y.E. to use your authority that Sig. Impresario pays Signora Girò at once not only the 6 zecchini but also the 20 lire for the copyist which I have to receive by rights. I hear the opera is long and it is certain that an opera lasting four hours was not suitable for Ferrara. Recomposing the recitatives I sincerely wanted to shorten them, but Lanzetti, by command of the impresario, hindered me from so doing.

ANT. VIVALDI

The only known formal portrait of
Vivaldi, often reproduced in the 18th
century, does not have the vitality
of Ghezzi's caricature.

The Basilica of San Marco was the centre of church music in Venice during Vivaldi's lifetime. Whether any of his own works were written for San Marco is uncertain, but the division of the chorus into two, which he uses, probably originated there. (Left) Choir singing from a huge music book, a drawing by Canaletto. (Below) The interior of the Basilica and (right) the Piazza in front of it as Vivaldi knew it.

Our most vivid literary portrait of Vivaldi comes from the dramatist Carlo Goldoni (above) *who as a young man was commissioned to rewrite the words of an aria in the opera 'Griselda' for him.*

(Right) *The Teatro S. Samuele, where the performance of 'Griselda' was due to take place.*

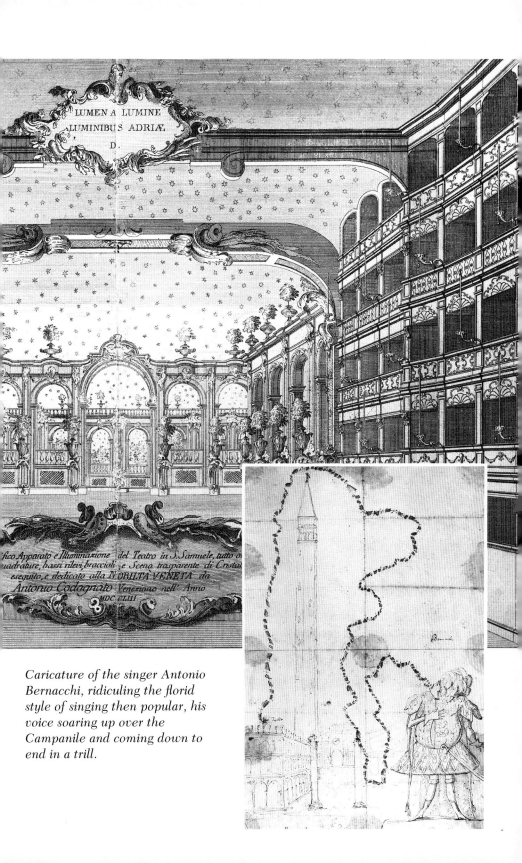

LUMEN A LUMINE
LUMINIBUS ADRIÆ
D.

fico Apparato e Illuminazione del Teatro in S. Samuele, tutto o...
uadrature, bassi rilevi, bracciali, e Scena trasparente di Cristal...
eseguito, e dedicato alla NOBILTÀ VENETA da
Antonio Codognato Veneziano nell' Anno
MDCCLIII.

Caricature of the singer Antonio Bernacchi, ridiculing the florid style of singing then popular, his voice soaring up over the Campanile and coming down to end in a trill.

BENEDICTUS MARCELLO
PATRITIUS VENETUS
Anno 1714 inter Academ Philarm cooptat obiit anno 1739

Four of Vivaldi's musical contemporaries. (Above left) George Frideric Handel, who wrote his opera 'Agrippina' in Venice in 1709. (Above) Benedetto Marcello, whose satire 'Il Teatro alla Moda' was perhaps in part directed against Vivaldi. (Left) Francesco Gasparini, Vivaldi's predecessor as music master of the Pietà (another caricature by Ghezzi).

(Right) Arcangelo Corelli, Vivaldi's older rival among Italian composers and like him patronized by Cardinal Ottoboni.

(Right) *Two examples of music printing showing the changes introduced during Vivaldi's lifetime. At the top, a page from his Opus 2 violin sonatas, each note being given its own tail. At the bottom, part of 'Winter' from 'The Four Seasons' printed by Estienne Roger of Amsterdam in the new style, with the tails joined up and written descriptions for the players incorporated.*

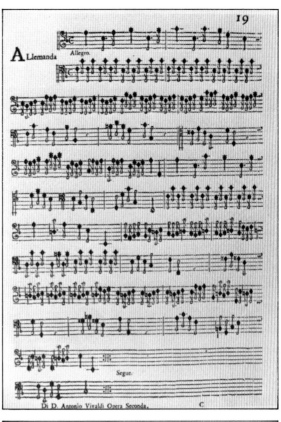

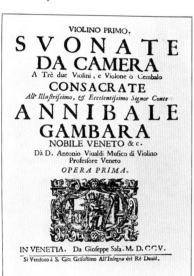

The title page of Vivaldi's Opus 1, published in Venice in 1705.

One of Vivaldi's letters to Guido Bentivoglio, dated 26 December 1736, a good example of his fine handwriting. He encloses part of the score of one of his operas and complains about the impresarios that he has to deal with. (For a full translation, see p. 133.)

Y.E. will have seen that I have written the truth about *la* Mancini and you will also share my opinion that *la* Moscovita is only a shadow of the former. Our theatres are in a bad way. They want me to do an opera for S. Cassiano for a fee of 100 zecchini, but my patrons and I are against it, because it is a badly run theatre and the tickets are so expensive that it is impossible to make a profit; therefore I can not risk my reputation.

I beg Y.E. for the revered continuation of your patronage etc.
Venice, 2 January 1737   Antonio Vivaldi

Meanwhile Lanzetti on 9 January had confirmed Vivaldi's additional expenses, only to retract the same on 12 January, wherein he states that these expenses were exaggerated and Vivaldi had forced him to write the letter of 9 January. It is understandable that the Marquis was beginning to find all these intrigues tiresome, to say the least ... He wrote to Vivaldi on 17 March 1737, stressing his estimation of the Girò sisters; but Vivaldi will also be welcome in Ferrara ... After an interval of nearly two months, Vivaldi reports from Verona on the great success of his new opera *Catone in Utica*, which after six performances has covered its costs. Proposals are made for a similar opera at Ferrara, but not at Carnival. Vivaldi hopes for an invitation as impresario.

Excellency. I repeat most humbly to Y.E. my old observation that also while in Verona I try to stay in your good graces. Here, thank God, my opera *Catone in Utica* [see Appendix I] is praised to the stars, there is nothing which will not please, whether the musicians or the dancers, everyone after his or her own merits. In this part of the country they do not love Intermezzi, therefore on many evenings they are suppressed. I am unhappy that Y.E., perhaps being obliged to leave for Bologna, will not be able to attend my opera, which I think you will find most splendidly done. We did only six performances and yet, having done all the accounts, I know for sure there will be no loss, on the contrary, if God blesses the stagione to the end, there will be a profit and not a negligible one.

A similar opera, composed moreover partly with a new text could, as I believe, attract a great audience also in Ferrara. It can not however be put on during Carnival; the ballet alone would cost me in the Carnival Season 700 Luigi [louis d'or], whereas in summer I can get them without difficulty for any price I want.

I am a frank contractor in similar cases and make use of my own capital and not with borrowed money. It would be enough if Y.E. command me or give me a sign that the idea pleases you, and I will give myself the honour of fulfilling your command.

Attending your most valued sign, I subscribe myself your humble etc.

Antonio Vivaldi

Verona, 3 May 1737

Bentivoglio replies on 5 May 1737, rejoicing with the composer over his success at Verona, but suggests to the composer not to take the new opera to Ferrara in the Autumn when Bentivoglio will be away.

In November Vivaldi resumes the correspondence. He is to supply an opera for the next Carnival at Ferrara, but is preoccupied by troubles over a ballerina named Coluzzi, who has fled her father and eloped with another dancer, Angelo Pompeati, of whom the composer disapproves. She intends to dance at Venice in the Autumn, and Vivaldi invokes Bentivoglio's help in preventing her from appearing in Venice rather than at Ferrara, where she ought to be by 2 December.

Excellency. As soon as Y.E.'s kindness gave me the pleasure of hoping for your patronage concerning my theatre in Ferrara, I present to you, with my deepest respect, a humble request. I engaged *la* Coluzzi – the contract written by her herself – that she will be there for all rehearsals and performances for a token sum of 100 Luigi [louis d'or], a sum she has never seen before. It will be known to Y.E. that she has escaped from her father. Now she wants to marry Pompeati, also a dancer, who will dance the coming Carnival in Turin, a very bad man inside and out, capable of every absurdity and whim. Even now one says that *la* Coluzzi would like to dance this autumn in Venice, something I will not negotiate with her, because to put together a ballet one needs nearly 16 to 18 days – not even in Venice can one do better –

because all the dancers are dispersed here and there and I arranged to attach them to Catenella, a good choreographer, who sometimes works together with Mme St. George. If *la* Coluzzi dances here in autumn, they have to put together the ballet in 5 or 6 days, and that is impossible. I hope that the Procuratessa Foscarini executes Y.E.'s commissions with great promptness and therefore I beg you humbly to do me the favour of writing an effective letter to the above mentioned lady that she will call *la* Coluzzi and order her to be in Ferrara on the second of December. What however is really most pressing on my mind is the kindness of Y.E. to write me the most courteous letters which show me how willingly you give me your patronage for my theatre. I beg you therefore to do me this favour. I leave the 15th. With the profoundest respect I remain etc.

Antonio Vivaldi

Venice, 6 November 1737

A week later the ballerina Coluzzi is still causing problems, but regardless of when she chooses to arrive in Ferrara, Vivaldi proposes to start the season on 26 December. He will leave Venice on 15 November.

Excellency. There is no end to the signs of the most generous gestures of kindness with which Y.E. favours me and I fear that the H.E. la Signora Procuratessa has never received your amicable commissions, but I must tell Y.E. that in all those days I was in agony if she would let *la* Coluzzi dance in S. Gio. Grisostomo [*sic*]. Cà Grimani had already discussed the affair with my Maestro Choreographer, that he may rehearse them even without *la* Coluzzi because she is capable of learning them in two days. The moment Y.E. condescended to assume that responsibility, I answered H.E. Michele Grimani that he should write to you, while I await for one of your revered signs; in fact I also believe that they are going to write, and Y.E. can facilitate the situation as much as you like, because by now I have assured myself that whatever time *la* Coluzzi comes I will start the performance on the day of S. Stefano [December 26], which date I would not neglect for a lot of money. Monday, may God will it, I

part for Ferrara, and in the meantime I and the ladies Girò
remain Y.E.'s most attached, devoted and humble servant
                                                     Antonio Vivaldi
Venice, 13 November 1737

The next item in the correspondence is Vivaldi's most famous,
autobiographical letter. The Cardinal of Ferrara, Tomaso Ruffo, has
suddenly interested himself in the operatic troupe in general and
Vivaldi in particular, suggesting that La Girò is Vivaldi's mistress
and that the composer refuses to say Mass. The contracts, involving
6000 ducats, are in danger. It is out of the question not to employ
Girò, or indeed Vivaldi himself. Perhaps Bentivoglio can persuade
Ruffo to cancel the whole opera season, in which case Vivaldi would
be able legally to avoid paying out the contracts.

Excellency. After many intrigues and troubles the opera in
Ferrara has tumbled to the ground. Today this Monsignore
Nunzio Apostolico summoned me and ordered me in the name of
H. Em. Ruffo not to come to Ferrara to perform the opera,
because I have a friendship with the singer Girò. Such a big blow;
Y.E. can imagine my state. I have on my shoulders the burden of
6000 ducats in contracts for this opera, and at present I have paid
out more than one hundred zecchini. It is impossible to give the
opera without *la* Girò, because one can not find a prima donna
like her. It is also impossible to do the opera without me, because
I will not entrust such a large sum to other hands. I am, moreover,
bound by the contracts; therefore, alas, I have a mountain of
difficulties. What grieves me most is that H. Em. Ruffo puts a
stain on these poor women which the world never gave them.

   For more than 14 years we have travelled together; we were
in many European cities, and everywhere their honesty was
admired, and one can say that also in Ferrara. Every week they
do their devotions, witnesses can swear to this, as one who is
sworn to one's faith should do.

   I have not said Mass for 25 years and will never do so, not
because I am forbidden to do so, as Y.E. can inform himself, but
through my own free will, because since birth I am afflicted by a

148

sickness. As a newly ordained priest, I said Mass only a little longer than a year, then I had to abstain, because I had to leave the altar three times without finishing the Mass on account of my illness. For that reason I nearly always stay at home, and if I go out only in a gondola or a coach, because I cannot walk, since I am afflicted by a narrowness in my chest and asthma. No gentleman would summon me to his house, not even our Prince, they are all informed of my defect. Immediately after the midday meal I can go out, but never on foot. That is the reason I do not celebrate Mass. I was for three Carnival seasons in Rome for the opera; and as Y.E. knows, I never said Mass; and I played the violin in the theatre and one knows that even His Holiness wanted to hear me play and I received many compliments.

I was called to Vienna where I did not say Mass. I was three years in Mantua in the service of the very pious Prince of Darmstadt; I was there with the two ladies who were always looked upon by His Highness with utmost benignity; and also there I never said Mass. My journeys are always very expensive, because I have to have always four or five persons with me to assist me. All which I can do well, I do at home and at the desk. For that reason I have the honour to correspond with nine princes of high rank and my letters travel throughout the whole of Europe. Therefore I have written to Signor Mazzuchi that I cannot come to Ferrara if he would not give me his house. In short, everything comes from that illness, and those ladies help me so much, because they are familiar with my distress.

This truth is known in nearly all of Europe; therefore I turn to the kindness of Y.E. that you condescend to inform also His Em. Ruffo, because this command is my total undoing. I repeat to Y.E. that without me one can not do the opera in Ferrara for the reasons that can be seen. If I can not put it on, I must take it to another place, which I can not organise now nor can I pay all the contracts, so that if His Eminence does not change his mind, I implore Y.E. to get at least from H. Em. Legato an order to cancel the opera, so that I can not be forced to pay out the contracts.

I also send to Y.E. the letters of H. Em. Albani which I should have presented myself. I have been a maestro in the Pietà for 30 years and always without any scandals. I recommend myself to the kind patronage of Y.E. and remain your most humble and obedient servant.

Antonio Vivaldi

Venice 16⁴ November 1737

Bentivoglio replies immediately, 20 November 1737. He informs the composer that the Cardinal will not change his mind regarding Vivaldi's presence as impresario at Ferrara. He cannot forbid the opera, for which there is no valid reason, particularly since plays will also be given during the Carnival season. Bentivoglio suggests that Vivaldi turn over the whole opera season to Picchi, a local impresario. He also suggests that it was not a good idea for Vivaldi to have sent Abbé Bollani to intercede with the Cardinal, who frowns on priests being involved with operatic productions. In reply Vivaldi again justifies his way of life. He agrees to use Picchi, but notes that the Girò sisters inhabit a separate house, 'far away from me.'

Excellency!

God will it! I can not add anything to Y.E. I can only assure Y.E. on my word of honour that it came into my head to go to Ferrara to do the opera and in the long run to be of some use to Y.E., my most benevolent protector.

His Eminence Ruffo does not take into consideration that I played in Rome and twice in the private apartements before the Pope. He puts that obstacle in my path and I must resign myself. Certainly, that opera can not be done without me in Ferrara. So as not to bother Y.E. any longer with long letters I will write Signor Picchij to keep you informed. His Eminence Ruffo is surely now well informed, perhaps because I handle my opera enterprises with too much delicacy.

I never wait at the door [i.e. to sell tickets] – I would be ashamed of myself – and in Ferrara I thought Picchij would do that. I never play in the orchestra, save the first night, because I do not condescend to become an orchestra musician. I never stay in the same house as the sisters Girò.

Malicious tongues may say what they want. Y.E. knows that in Venice I have my house for which I pay 200 ducats and the Girò ladies have another far away from me. I will stop writing because

I must lay myself at H.E. the Marchese Rondinelli's feet and I remain Y.E.'s

most humblest, obedient etc. servant

Venice 23 November 1737   Antonio Vivaldi

A week later, Vivaldi finds Picchi's counter-proposals 'laughable'. He hopes that Bentivoglio will read Picchi this letter.

Excellency,
I think that Y.E. has been informed about everything by Signor Picchij. The propositions he made me are laughable. If I could have cheaper musicians and dancers, I would have – one must believe me – reserved them for myself. I assure Y.E. that those opera ensembles would have cost anybody else not 15,000 but 24,000 lire.

I have postponed my decisions until today, but if I was ruined in the end by time I can not cheat the others, the more since I have engaged musicians from as far away as Rome.

I am so sorry that the main reason for all that was my wish to be of service to Y.E. I implore Y.E. to blame my adverse fate and to believe that I will try whenever and wherever possible, to lay my respect at your feet and remain Y.E.'s

obsequious, most humble and most submissive servant

Antonio Vivaldi

Venice, 30 November 1737

P.S. There is no time to say it again. After I had written all the letters I thought of an express messenger as a means to learn of the decisions Wednesday morning from Ferrara, but that would cost me 9 zecchini. Picchij makes many mistakes in his accounts. I beg nevertheless Y.E. to have him read my letter and also excuse [my] boldness.

The next letter concerns the engagement of a soprano and a castrato.

Excellency,
I have had the honour of obeying Y.E.'s most valued orders even

151

before having received them. H.E. the Ambassador was kind enough to inform me that he has written to Y.E. He has presented to me, and allowed me to hear, the soprano whom I found attractive, with a good voice and proper school. Hence I have forestalled your orders, but at the same time stressing carefully the high respect I maintain towards Y.E.'s name, and in my total devotion to have the honour to search out every route to satisfy your every wish, I caused the impresario to engage the castrato [*Musico*].

I pray Y.E.'s goodness to find me worthy of new orders, to enable me with renewed courage to kiss your hands and to assure you, together with the Girò ladies, of my most humble respects and remain,

Y.E.'s most humbled and obedient servant
Antonio Vivaldi

Venice, 9 November 1738

At Ferrara, Vivaldi's *Siroe*, the first opera of the season, was a disastrous failure and they are now proposing not to stage *Farnace*, the second opera specially revised for Ferrara. There was objection to his recitatives, which Vivaldi, considering that he has composed 94 operas, refuses to countenance. There are difficulties over Berretta, the first harpsichordist, who altered Vivaldi's recitatives. Vivaldi hopes that Bentivoglio will intervene.

Excellency,

If the unhappy have no protection from the most exalted of Maecenos, they sink into desperation. In such a miserable state am I now, if Y.E., my long suffering patron, does not come to my aid. My reputation in Ferrara is scourged in such a way that they refuse to stage *Farnace* as the second opera which was put newly together by me for the company according to the contract I had with Mauro. My greatest crime is, one says, that my recitatives are impossible. With my name, my reputation throughout the whole of Europe, and having composed in any case 94 operas, I can not support such accusations therefore I have the honour of informing Y.E. of the whole truth.

After all the stories I heard I was already sure that Beretta [Pietro Antonio Berretta, *Maestro di Cappella* at Ferrara

Cathedral] was not up to playing the first harpsichord, but Signor Acciaioli assured me that he [Berretta] was a good artist and an honourable man, although I found him later on a foolhardy simpleton. Even after the first rehearsals I heard that when accompanying the recitatives he had no idea what he was doing; then he had the audacity to tamper with my recitatives and they are now bad, as a result of his changes and his inability to execute them.

The truth is, they are the same recitatives which were done without changing a note in Ancona and Y.E. knows how much they were highly applauded, even some scenes on account of the recitatives.

The same were sung during the rehearsals in Venice by Michielino, second tenor in Ferrara, and went admirably, and if they will be sung by Michielino during the main rehearsals one will then see if they are good or bad. The main thing is that in my originals not a note was removed, either with a knife nor with a pen, from which it follows that everything which was done is the work of that wonderful artist.

Excellency, I am desperate, I can not bear that such an ignoramus makes his fortune on the ruin of my poor name. I humbly beseech you not to forsake me, because I swear to Y.E., if my reputation is at stake I shall take action to defend my honour, for he who takes my honour from me, takes my life. The highest protection of Y.E. is my only solace in that case, and kissing your hand with tearful eyes I remain resigned to my fate. I remain,

Y.E.'s most humble and devoted servant

Antonio Vivaldi

2 January 1739
P.S. All those difficulties arise because I am not in Ferrara and Monsignore the Commissionaire staunchly believes in the impresario.

Bentivoglio's last letter to Vivaldi is dated 7 January 1739. The Marquis sympathises with the composer but is patently unwilling to become involved any further.

A curious coda to this exchange of letters was recently discovered in the Venetian archives.[5] Antonio Mauro had been engaged as a painter for the theatre decorations at Ferrara. Vivaldi evidently asked him to leave for Ferrara at short notice and to pay Vivaldi's debts. Mauro's writ (below) was intended to force Vivaldi to pay sums of money which Mauro considered were owed to him.

Scrittura Extragiudiziale
On Wednesday the 4th March of the year 1739 after the birth of our Lord Jesus Christ; second protocol for the files. Presented by and in the name of Antonio Mauro with the purpose to include it in my file and to deliver as stated herein.

Since I, Antonio Mauro, was forced by your repeated requests which you, Reverend Don Antonio Vivaldi, put to me, that I should just for appearances and never to harm my own interests – because it would never be right and proper that I should suffer any disadvantage or be in any form molested – sign and confirm certain contracts of singers, dancers, musicians and others, [contracts] which were already arranged by yourself beforehand and agreed upon, that is to say during the year 1738 for the opera in Ferrara, when you were the one and only lord and master, which is absolutely true, since I was only a painter, engaged to execute the commissioned decorations.

But as the situation arises, to guard my honour and to honour truth I am forced to present to you, Reverend Don Vivaldi, the following extrajudicial document attested by Signor Iseppo Mozoni, notary in Venice that, if at any time and for whatever reason I should have any disadvantage through my signing the contracts which you had made, that you should shield me as it is only fair and just – from private or judicial claims because only through your repeated entreaties I left suddenly at a few hours notice for Ferrara. You gave me a bill of payment with which I should pay your liabilities, as you know. Should you be of a different opinion (which I can not believe) I would be forced to present myself at those courts which would guard my advantage and do justice to my needs and also will give me advice – when I tell them about the tricks you used to cheat me, when I was only carrying out your wishes. That much will be told to you and you are notified by this document that you can not deny my interest and also my requirement made known to you and that you should provide for me, so that, considering justice and reason, I am not the loser.

It will be your duty to consider your obligations, otherwise it will be my duty to find such means as to convince you and to reveal your trickery and your dealings which neither God nor the world can applaud. That much etc.

Next day. The bailiff Giacomo Cuppis reported to have consigned against receipt the above mentioned document entire and complete to the Reverend Don Antonio Vivaldi in whose house it was given to a woman, as stated above.

What follows is Vivaldi's answer to the above writ. Mauro's position was secured by Vivaldi, replacing Girolamo Lechi, impresario of the Ferrara Opera, who was removed from the post. Vivaldi accuses Mauro of having absconded with 300 scudi of bad debts from the Ferrara situation. Vivaldi enumerates all the favours, financial and otherwise, he has showered on Mauro, who owes money to the musicians, dancers and the composer himself.

Scrittura Extragiudiziale

Since I, Antonio Vivaldi was forced by You, Antonio Mauro, with your repeated requests during a whole month (as can be verified by witnesses) to remove nearly with bodily force Girolamo Lech [*sic*] from the Ferrara enterprise, whose legal and confirmed impresario he was and who was also trusted to run the theatre (as one can see from the letters) in order to provide you with a position, I would never have thought that, trying to cleanse yourself of any fault, you would stoop so low as to initiate a law suit by charging me such a disreputable document, considering that it was I who was only attempting to do you a favour and seeking a way to extricate yourself from your misery which I knew only too well, in that – as you well know – one lent you in my house an *andrienne* dress [costume first worn by actress Doncourt in *Andria*, Paris 1703] which you could pledge for financial help.

Do you really believe that all are dead who played and danced in Ferrara? That all the contracts and agreements you signed with your own hand were destroyed? That all the letters you wrote me were burnt? Which crazy brain gave you such bad advice to write me such an absurd document? It would have been much better to stick to your twisted neck and your easy tears asking for compassion, protesting your innocence as you did in Ferrara. Perhaps your creditors would have given you the 300 scudi with which you defrauded the enterprise and with which you fled.

I, as you know well, was always well disposed to you and would not for long have withstood your crocodile tears. You know, as does the whole of Venice, how many thousand of ducats I paid you during the years you were in my service in the theatre. Do you believe I have lost the letters you wrote me saying that Francesco Picchi in Ferrara had persisted with all his might that you relinquish the enterprise, which you resisted, because the earnings were secure and plentiful.

Remember that I have the answer to that letter of mine in which I urged you and tried to persuade you that you should leave the enterprise, since you would earn 150 scudi and more through your work as stage designer and light specialist; that I also wrote that, if you would not step down, you would not be my friend any more and no longer deserved that God help you. Remember that I have those letters written by your hand with all those ridiculous and unjustified demands when you were forced out. It is well known that, when you left Venice, you left behind all your qualms of conscience and with the idea to use the enterprise for your own ends. You thought it wise to cooperate with the above-mentioned experienced Picchi, so that you could divide the cake after your own taste and leave the poor musicians, dancers and the conductor to their empty stomachs. You played your cards so badly that you had to pawn the necklace in question which you pretend belongs to your recent wife. And after your return from Ferrara you and your nephew not only had a new wardrobe, you also ransomed the necklace; you paid 25 ducats for a new staircase in your house, bought expensive furniture, laid in stores of wine and flour; all that is known and can be proved.

It would behove you to think about your duty and remember that your slanders and your cheating will not absolve you from paying the musicians, dancers and myself. Remember that unthankfulness is a dastardly sin, subterfuges are an imputation of the devil to cover up the truth.

And remember once more that God sees, God knows and God judges [all] and that you, apart from facing the holy judgement of the Serenissima, have to answer God in everything. So much etc.

This submitted document belongs to the files of Signor Giovanni Domenico Redolfi, notary in Venice.

Thursday, the 12th of March 1739. Through the worthy Sig. Marco Lezze, solicitor, in the name of S. Abbate Don Antonio Vivaldi. This document is presented for distribution as indicated. Friday, the 13th inst. The bailiff Signor Iseppo Treve stated to have delivered the above mentioned letter entire and completely to Signor Antonio Mauro and had given the document to a man in the house against receipt, as it was the wish of the above mentioned Signor Abbate Don Antonio Vivaldi.

Finally Mauro maintains at some length that he took over the Carnival season at Ferrara in 1738 only because of Vivaldi's insistence, and not as impresario but simply as stage designer. In order to travel to Ferrara, Mauro has to pawn his wife's jewelry for 20 ducats. Vivaldi still owes Mauro 'a not unimportant sum'.

Scrittura Extragiudiziale
Monday the 16th of March 1739, second report for the files, presented by and in the name of Signor Antonio Mauro to be included into the file and handed over as noted herein.

That which one can read in the document you, Reverend Don Antonio Vivaldi, had composed and Signor Zan Domenego Redolfi, notary in Venice, has delivered to the files and also to me Antonio Mauro this month is one of the usual scribblings full of false statements, which I will nevertheless refute with serious protestations. Since you say it is known that to manage an opera during the Carnival this past year 1738 was only done due to your repeated insistence, that the execution of those contracts concluded and confirmed by you without my knowledge was done by me obeying your orders, even when you knew that I did not strive for the position of Impresario, but was only interested to get a position – as anybody would try – as stage designer for the sets intended for you, and then you do not even visit the stage while you spread the word that these were your ideas, but one could not accommodate your wishes because they went against those of the people of Ferrara.

Far from the truth is the damaging remark made by you, Don Vivaldi, in the document of the 13th of this month that I had caused in the year of 1738 the expulsion of Signor Gerolamo Lechi from the opera in Ferrara to place myself in his position during the time, when only you were capable of putting me there. One should state that you took care to involve in the above mentioned enterprise not only Signor Antonio Denzio but also Signor Antonio Abatti; both were adamant not to let you use their names and even after you promised them many things, which obligations I should undertake to fulfil, you could not persuade them even then when you told them that you would take care of the selection of agreements and provide contracts for the musicians, dancers and so on. All your promises came to nothing and therefore you tried desperately to have me act as (as albeit pseudo) impresario at the time when I was only your representative and never could be more than that, so that I could keep you abreast by letter about your affairs and to wait until I could convey the aforesaid news to you.

The reproach that Signora Paulina Girò, whom you then knew very well, lent me three years ago an *andriè* [andrienne] dress so that I could pawn it for 16 Philippi for my trip to Pesaro, has nothing to do with this matter; that story will not serve you in this particular dispute. If she lent it to me, I made sure to return it in a few days. You should reflect on my poverty at that time as I then wrote you, and not with a twisted neck but an open brow. And here lies the responsibility you have accepted to better my poor state and to take care that the singers and the other people to whom you are bound contractually be considered in the situation for which you were responsible.

It is risible – although not a witty joke – if you maintain that I bought furniture, paid debts and redeemed pawns, when I did that for you. When I had to travel to Ferrara you had no money, so that I was forced to pawn the jewelry of my wife for 20 ducats and after my return I had to pawn something else to redeem [the jewelry], and not with money from Ferrara but my own. And when I paid bills for me and that house I live in, it is not your business to concern yourself with the means used for that purpose. And if you can not put anything else in the document, except that I had laid my hands on the money of Ferrara, it would be better to spare your quill, since those invented inculpations are not only wrong, but of no use to you. And just as wrong is also your statement that I wanted to quit the theatre since it was not in my power to do that without your will. You had better acknowledge that all those who wanted to get involved in that affair fled like the devils when sighting the holy water, when they were informed by the contracting parties. It would have been your duty, I say, my dearest Signor Vivaldi, to ponder the just settlement of that affair, to which your conscience holds you, about the agreements and the contracts, and not to bring up touching stories (which you always like to do) which have nothing to seek in court and are moreover far from the truth and also state that during your time when you managed other well-known theatres, you caused me to earn a lot of money; if I got it, I got it for my work and for that you still owe me a not unimportant sum which I did not demand so as not to have to deal with the Reverend Vivaldi. But I would hope that you would reflect a little more on the whole affair as it now presents itself and that in case of need you would protect me against the demands accruing from the contracts and also that you will not give cause for more documents outside the law courts, since this present one should serve as a protest against any law costs which I, Antonio Mauro, may have to pay to you.

This statement is herewith registered and communicated to you without prejudice.

It must have been increasingly clear to Vivaldi that his position in Italy was becoming untenable. We have no idea when the composer began to turn his eye to northern Europe, on the other side of the Alps; but there was still Venice and Vivaldi was not going to abandon his mother city without one last effort. And so we open the last chapter of Vivaldi's life in the lagoon city.

XII

The Last Journey: Death in Vienna

❧

A last grand season for Vivaldi at the San Angelo Theatre in 1738 brought three new works, two of them pasticcios. The first was *L'oracolo in Messenia*, entirely by Vivaldi; then there was *Armida al campo d'Egitto*, now twenty years old and revised as a pasticcio; while the third was *Rosmira*, another pasticcio. It almost seems as if Vivaldi was gradually being manoeuvered into a position where he was more highly admired as an operatic 'editor' or 'arranger' than as an original composer. There followed in 1739 Vivaldi's last San Angelo opera, *Feraspe*, which had been preceded with Ancona's production of *Siroe, rè di Persia*, a revival of 1727, which was yet another pasticcio arranged by the composer. Vivaldi's operas were no longer fashionable. One revival never made the stage at all.

Vivaldi dedicated the original libretto of *Rosmira fedele* to Frederick Margrave of Brandenburg, with whom the composer was in touch.

> Most Serene Highness,
> whatever is the tribute which in my most devoted respect I offer Your Highness with joyful temerity, I hope that you will esteem it, because I do not measure Princes with the same merits as yours. You are distinguished by virtue of the greatness of your heart, whereas the others find their pleasures in the small bagatelles they are given. Receive therefore, Magnanimous, this drama which flowed from the felicitious pen of the celebrated Silvio Stampiglia with the dedication from me to you, not to show in the former deeds of some hero the signs of your future since you have no need for the examples of others since you have in

160

YOUR GREAT FAMILY so many and illustrious ones. The glory of your Father and your Ancestors suffice and you have enough advantages through your birth and your inclinations, not to need to look for deeds in past history or among foreign nations. This opera is composed to entertain, for occasionally great Princes also find pleasure in the quality of those graceful entertainments which lighten their spirits, burdened by the cares of Government. This is my intent; and happy shall I be if that purpose be attained; together with the pardon for my daring, always enviable even if it be considered a fault – because such a fault will always be thought noble if it gives me the pleasure to lay at Your Highness's feet my profoundest respect, calling myself Your Highness's most humble, devoted and obedient servant,

Antonio Vivaldi

There were plans to stage *Tito Manlio* at San Angelo again; Giazotto found a *faccio fede*, the petition to gain official permission to stage the work dated 27 January 1739.[1] But it was too late for Vivaldi. An opera by Hasse was given instead.

It would seem that Venice was no longer a centre for Vivaldi. But abroad his was still a name to conjure with, and he was invited to participate in a ceremony at Amsterdam, where the governors of the theatre had decided to celebrate their centenary. On 7 January 1738 the spectacle took place, produced by Vivaldi himself, in person. There were the usual plays and a big programme of music: nine *sinfonie* for strings (two by Giovanni Chinzer, and one each by Johann Agrell, his pupil Bernard Hubfeld, Wilhelm de Fesch, Andrea Temanza, and three others which can no longer be identified).

All this was preceded by a 'concerto Grosso à 10 Stromenti, due corni da caccia, tympano, due oboe, violino principale, due violini, alto-viola con basso' (RV 562a). The harpsichord continuo was played by Jan Ulhoorn, and Vivaldi led, presumably as solo violinist.[2]

It was a signal honour from a city which had brought forth the *corpus* of Vivaldi's published music: now, the centre of music publishing was to switch to Paris for the next half-a-century.

Back in Venice in 1739, the Pietà put on a piece entitled *Mopso* ('egloga pescatoria a cinque voce', 'piscatorial ecologue with five voices') which Vivaldi conducted in the presence of Ferdinand of Bavaria, brother of the Elector Charles Albert. The prince had particularly requested to hear a performance of the Pietà girls and especially appreciated the cantata, singling out the 'brilliant accompaniment' of the orchestra ... which had always constituted the chief adornment of the institution.' Vivaldi was not only honoured but given presents by the visiting nobles.[3]

On 29 August 1739, President de Brosses wrote from Venice to M. de Blancey:

Vivaldi has become my intimate friend for the purpose of selling me some very expensive concertos. He was partly successful in this, and I was successful for my part too, which was to hear him and enjoy good and frequent musical recreations. He is an old man [*vecchio*], who has a fury of prodigious composition.

I have heard him vaunt his ability to compose a concerto in all its parts more swiftly than a copyist could copy it. I found to my great surprise that he was not so esteemed as he merits in this country, where all is *mode* [fashion], where his music has been about for a long time and the music of last year no longer earns money.

Benedetto Marcello, who was to die in the province of Istria on 24 July 1739, wrote three years earlier to a friend[4] '... Illustrious and young friend, all has changed in Venice, nothing is celebrated but vice and there is no longer a passion for noble things, for science and art which are the prerogatives of a strong people ... Today I have the time to meditate on the many sadnesses which make up life in my city ...'. It was time, the 'red priest' may have thought, to leave the lagoon city.

But before doing so, however, there were things to be completed, first a grand concert at the Pietà. On 19 December 1739 Prince Frederick Christian, son of Frederick Augustus, King of Poland and Elector of Saxony, arrived in Venice. He had journeyed there from Naples, where lived his sister, married to Don Carlos, the future Carlos III of Spain who was to achieve posthumous immortality through Goya's famous portraits of him and his family. In Venice, he was escorted by four noblemen who looked after his needs at the Palazzo Foscarini. Prince Frederick Christian enjoyed all the tourist sights – glass-blowing on the nearby island of Murano, bull fights, visits to the churches – and three musical performances, one at the Pietà (21 March), one at the Mendicanti (29 March) and one at the Incurabili (4 April). The opening one at the Pietà, for which the hall was hung with gold brocade and damask, was a Cantata, *Il Coro delle Muse*, a pasticcio, for which Vivaldi composed a *sinfonia* (RV 149), and in which sang the young ladies Apollonia, la Bolognese, Giulietta, Ambrosina, Fortunata, Chiaretta, Margherita, Teresa and Albetta.

There was also a notable contribution, otherwise, by Vivaldi. The Sächsische Landesbibliothek in Dresden owns a volume entitled:

Concertos for several instruments played by the girls of the charitable asylum of the Pietà before His Royal Highness the Most Serene Frederick Christian, Royal Prince of Poland and Electoral Prince of Saxony. Music by Don Antonio Vivaldi, *maestro de'concerti* at the aforesaid asylum. In Venice in the year 1740.

[Concerti con molti Istromenti Suonati dalle Figlie del Pio Ospitale della Pietà avanti Sua Altezza Reale Il Serenissimo Federico Cristiano Prencipe Reale di Polonia et Elettorale di Sassonia. Musica di D. Antonio Vivaldi Maestro de Concerti dell'Ospitale Sudetto. In Venezia nell'anno 1740.]

At the end of the first part of the Cantata, the libretto informs us, 'Segue Concerto di Viola d'Amore, e Leuto col ripieno di moltissimi Strumenti' – the third of the Dresden volume (which includes RV 540, 552 and 558). At the end of the second part, 'Segue il Concerto a Violini obbligati con Eco', the second of the Dresden volume. Pincherle[5] identified in the Pietà archives the sums paid for these four pieces: Vivaldi received on 27 April fifteen ducats and thirteen lire 'for three concertos and a sinfonia'; another document specifies 'Antonio Vivaldi maestro di concerti per haver composto tre concerti ed una sinfonia ... duc[ati] 15. 13.'

And so Vivaldi, now an old gentleman of sixty-two, began what would be his final journey – to Vienna, where he obviously expected patronage from his old admirer Charles VI or – depending upon the exact date he set out from Venice – Francis Stephen, the future Emperor, for whom Vivaldi had been a 'foreign' *maestro di cappella* on his operatic librettos from 1735, when Francis Stephen was Grand Duke of Tuscany. Before leaving, he obviously wanted the Pietà to purchase a sizeable collection of his music, which at first they were rather reluctant to do.[6]

> In consideration of the fact that our Choro needs concertos for organ and other instruments to maintain its present reputation and having heard, moreover, that Rev. Vivaldi is about to leave these domains, and has a goodly portion of concertos ready and willing to be sold: it is therefore moved that the Governors in charge of the Choro be empowered to purchase them in real ducats, at the rate of one each.
>
> Abstentions ....3 ⎤
> Against...........................3 ⎬ motion not carried[11]
> For ....4 ⎦

Put again, the motion failed to pass; but something seems to have changed their minds, for on 12 May 1740 Vivaldi was paid seventy ducats and twenty-three lire for twenty concertos (another receipt in the Pietà archives mentions 440 lire or 22 ducats).

One of the last-known affairs with which Vivaldi was associated concerned yet another operatic failure. In a recently discovered document we learn that the composer was ordered to give evidence in the case of non-payment of the singers for the staging of his opera *Feraspe*, which as we have seen was given in the autumn at San Angelo in Venice under the impresario Felice Dini. He was asked on 24 May 1740 to provide a statement concerning his fee as composer, but when the authorities attempted to deliver this summons, the neighbours stated that Vivaldi was out of town. If it be assumed that the officers of the Pietà wished to pay Vivaldi in person – and not a deputy – for his sale of the twenty concertos on 20 May 1740, the composer's departure for Austria can be fixed between 12 and 24 May 1740.

It is likely that Vivaldi accompanied Anna Giraud to Graz, where she sang in his *Catone in Utica* (autumn 1740); perhaps in 1739 as well.

Whatever Vivaldi's hopes were for Vienna and Charles VI, the Emperor died in October 1740 after eating a plate of poisonous mushrooms. Maria Theresa and her consort Francis Stephen assumed power, and no doubt Vivaldi and his problems were very far from their minds: the political situation in Austria, and relations with Frederick The Great and Prussia were tense – but that is another story.

We learn of Vivaldi's presence in Vienna because of an autograph receipt of 28 June 1741 for the sale of compositions to Antonio Vinciguerra, Count of Collalto, a Venetian nobleman whose principle residence in Moravia was the Castle at Brtnice:[7]

This 28 June 1741

Vienna

I, the undersigned, acknowledge receipt of twelve Hungarian [florins] from the hon. secretary of H.S.H. Ant:° Vig:ª Count of Collalto for settling the account of, and on the orders of H.S.H., a purchase of much music sold by me, valued at —— Fl. 12.

I Ant:° Vivaldi affirm the above in my own hand

(Moravian Museum, Brno)

It is the final document we have from Vivaldi's hand, and may account for the presence of many unique works attributed to the composer now in Moravian and Bohemian archives. e.g. the *Salve Regina* (RV 617) in F, also in the Brno Museum.

A month later the 'red priest' was dead. He had been living in the house of a saddler's widow named Waller or Wahler – *das Sattlerische Haus*, on the Kärntnerstrasse (the house no longer exists). It was 28 July 1741. The cause of death was listed as 'innerlicher Brand' (literally 'internal inflammation', which tells us nothing at all about the real cause of death). He was buried on that same day in the Hospital Cemetery (now destroyed). His funeral services, reproduced in facsimile from the archives of Saint Stephen's Cathedral, Vienna, by Pincherle and Kendall,[8] list costs of nineteen florins (gulden) and forty-five kreuzer; he was entitled only to the *Kleingeläut*, or the pauper's peal of bells, costing two florins and thirty-six kreuzer. There were six pall-bearers and six choirboys from the parish church where Vivaldi died, which happened to be St Stephen's Cathedral. The six members of the *Cantorei* of St Stephen's included the young Joseph Haydn, who was thus probably one of the few to witness the demise of this great composer, now a pauper and already forgotten, placed, like Mozart half a century later, in an ignominious and anonymous grave somewhere under the great capital city of the Austrian Monarchy.[9]

At the request of the composer's two sisters, the *censori* in Venice ordered on 3 September 1741 that Vivaldi's house be sealed and his furniture removed beforehand. This should ensure, it was believed, the sisters' claim for housekeeping expenses and would avoid fraudulent speculation on the part of any would-be creditors. This injunction, incidentally, is the earliest known document from which we can deduce that news of Vivaldi's death in far-away Vienna had reached the lagoon city.[10]

o   o   o

When Vivaldi's death became known in Venice, there was a report in the *Commemorali Gradenigo*: '173 . . . l'Abbé D. Antonio Vivaldi, incomparable virtuose du violin, dit le Prêtre roux, très estimé pour ses compositions et concertos, avait gagné, en un temps, plus de 50,000 ducats, mais sa prodigalité desordonnée l'a fait mourir pauvre, à Vienne' ('173 . . . Abbé Lord Antonio Vivaldi, incomparable virtuoso of the violin, known as the Red Priest, much esteemed for his compositions and concertos, who earned more than 50,000 ducats in this life, but his disorderly prodigality caused him to die a pauper in Vienna.')[11]

EPILOGUE
The Durazzo Connection

꡾

At Vivaldi's death, the musical world, if it interested itself in the composer at all, counted the *oeuvres* as those published in Amsterdam and, later, Paris. The operas had all been forgotten and none had ever been printed in Vivaldi's lifetime. Those who knew the Pietà must have gathered that that institution owned a gigantic collection of instrumental and religious music by the composer in manuscript, but probably no one quite realized the enormous number of the red priest's works which had never been published. As we now know, the unpublished far outnumbered the published.

The history of how this vast collection of music disappeared and then dramatically re-appeared has all the elements of a spy chase. It is, in any case, well documented and we shall try to tell it in summary form: actually a whole book could be made out of this incredible tale, which spans the eighteenth, nineteenth and twentieth centuries and ends with the Ricordi publication of the complete instrumental music and the complete religious music (now, 1991, almost completed), which will carry us into the twenty-first century.[1]

The story begins in Vienna in 1749, where Count Giacomo Durazzo, of an old Genoese family, was appointed to be the Ambassador of his city-state to the Imperial Court. Durazzo married a Freifrau von Weissenwolff from a family who had intermarried with the Esterházys. Durazzo soon became a friend of the then reigning Prince Paul Anton Esterházy who later, in 1761, engaged Haydn as Vice-Kapellmeister. Meanwhile Durazzo made a spectacular career in Austria, becoming director of the Court Theatre in June 1754 and encouraging Calzabigi and Gluck. Under Durazzo's regime, Vienna saw the first performance of the epoch-making

*Silhouette of Count
Giacomo Durazzo when
Imperial Ambassador in
Venice.*

ballet *Don Juan* in 1761 and a year later the equally epoch-making
opera *Orfeo*. At this period, Durazzo became involved with the new
theatre in Eisenstadt and was appointed one of the principal
advisors in its reconstruction, thus coming into close contact with
Haydn. In 1765, the Empress Maria Theresa appointed Durazzo to
be the Austrian Ambassador to Venice, where he settled in a large
palazzo containing its own theatre, becoming one of the leading
musical and political forces until his death on 15 October 1794. We
know that he began to collect Haydn and corresponded with the
composer, and since by this time Vivaldi's music was almost totally
forgotten, Durazzo seems to have persuaded the board of the
Ospedale della Pietà, where Vivaldi had been music master and to
whom he had sold a large collection of his manuscripts before
leaving on what would be his final journey to Vienna, to sell this
intrinsically valuable collection to Durazzo. Durazzo then managed
to get hold of a large part of Vivaldi's Venetian opera scores. This
meant in the event that the Count was the owner of a large part of
Vivaldi's religious music (this from the Pietà), his unpublished
concertos and other instrumental music (also from the Pietà and
forming an enormous bulk), as well as secular vocal music (probably
from the Pietà) apart from the operas.

When the Napoleonic Wars burst upon Italy, it seemed that the
great Durazzo collection was divided into two parts. One part

remained in the family's possession in Genoa, and the other was given to the Monastery of Monferrato situated in the Lombard Plains. Neither the monks in Monferrato nor the Durazzo heirs in Genoa had the faintest idea of the importance of their respective collections.

In the confusion of the Napoleonic Wars, it appears that the musical library of the Court Orchestra at Turin was hidden when the court fled to Sardinia, and when peace finally returned, no one could remember where the hiding place was. For years, scholars and musicians hoped to rediscover its whereabouts, and the key man in our story turned out to be Professor Alberto Gentili of Turin University. In 1926, Gentili was summoned by a colleague from the Biblioteca Nazionale in Turin. The National Library had been offered a collection of musical manuscripts from the Monastery of Monferrato. It was the period when many great monastic houses in Europe had decided to sell some of their precious books or manuscripts to pay for much needed repairs. The Benedictine Monastery of Melk sold their Gutenberg Bible to pay for re-roofing the monastery; the monks at Monferrato found that they had a large musical library which had been left to them by a member of the Durazzo family and they thought to sell it to the National Library in Turin to help pay for repairs. The collection comprised ninety-five volumes, fourteen of them by Vivaldi. Alas, however, the Turin Library had no money for the acquisition. By this time an antiquarian dealer was involved as the agent, and Professor Gentili realized that, if he were to save the collection, he would have to raise the money from some outside source. He found such a source in the person of the Turin banker, Roberto Foà, who bought the manuscripts and donated them to the library in memory of his son Mauro who had died in childhood. The bequest was made in February 1927 and a year later Gentili presented to the musical world a selection of music from this new treasure trove.

From the way in which the Vivaldi volumes were numbered, Gentili saw that Monferrato Monastery had only received half the former Durazzo collection. There now began a frantic search for the remaining half, frantic because the antiquarian world was now hot on the trail as well. Gentili secured a member of the Italian aristocracy who was a geneological expert to try to trace members of the Durazzo family, and they soon found the actual nephew of the Durazzo who had left half of his music library to Monferrato. This nephew, Marquis Giuseppe Maria Durazzo, who lived in Genoa, was enraged when he heard that the monks had sold their part of the library and he refused to let anyone examine his own library. The Marquis's Father Confessor, a Jesuit, was then tracked down and after a certain amount of time, it was he who persuaded Durazzo to allow his library to be examined. Gentili found all the missing volumes and hastened back to Turin to raise more money for their purchase. He found a textile manufacturer named Filippo Giordano who, like Foà, had lost a son, Renzo, and in his name the next bequest was organized. On 30 January 1930 the Durazzo collection was united in the shelves of the Biblioteca Nazionale. The Marchese Durazzo had, however, stipulated that the music of this collection should never be published. There then ensued a huge legal battle which, fortunately, was lost by Durazzo and in 1936 the secretary of the Accademia Musicale Chigiana in Siena, Miss Olga Rudge, published a catalogue to the Durazzo collection – now of course called, and rightly, the Foà/Giordano bequest. The way to a thorough investigation of Vivaldi was opened.[2]

Appendices
Notes on the Text
Select Bibliography
Index
List of Illustrations

The opening of the soprano aria 'Con cento [e] cento bacci' from the opera 'La verità in cimento' (1720). This partly autograph ms. is signed by the composer in his usual manner – 'del Vivaldi' – in the upper right corner. The music is written in a scribal hand, while the vocal line, tempo, instrumental annotations and corrections are in the hand of the composer.

APPENDIX I
Vivaldi's Opera Productions

This brilliant catalogue of Vivaldi operas was prepared by the German scholar Reinhard Strohm: 'Vivaldi's career as an opera producer,' pp. 11ff. of Antonio Vivaldi, Teatro Musicale, Cultura e Società, published, appropriately, by the Fondazione Cini and the Istituto Italiano Antonio Vivaldi (Florence, 1982, two volumes). It is one of the most important contributions to our knowledge of Vivaldi to appear in recent decades. It includes not only operas with music by Vivaldi, but also those written by other composers for which he acted as impresario.

It has been brought up to date, using new research, by Sylvie Mamy in a recent study, 'La diaspora dei cantanti veneziani nella prima metà del settecento', in Nuovi Studi Vivaldiani, Edizione e Chronologia critica delle Opere (ed. Antonio Fanna & Giovanni Morelli, 2 vols., Florence 1988, Vol. II, pp. 591–631). We have, of course, incorporated these vital changes in our list, below. Using Reinhard Strohm as the basis, the changes by Sylvie Mamy are added underneath the original Strohm listing, and the numbers refer to her list.

Abbreviations: L = libretto; M = Mamy (see above); aut = autonno (autumn); car = carnivale; pri = primavera (spring); est = estate (summer); impr = impressum (printer); maggio = May; ded = dedicated to; (= 1727) means first performed in that year.

I Full opera seasons with control of theatre	II One-opera seasons with control of theatre	III Scritture with some control or influence	IV Scritture without control
1713 Orlando furioso aut, S. Ang. L: G. Braccioli (dedica) Music: G.A. Ristori M: 21, Braunschweig 1722 (M: 23, Prague 1724; M: 27, Mantua 1725; M: 60, Brno [Brünn] 1735; M: 68, Bergamo [q.v.]; M: 78, Bassano, 1741)		1713 Ottone in Villa maggio, Vicenza L: D. Lalli (dedica) M: 1	

I	II	III	IV
Full opera seasons with control of theatre	One-opera seasons with control of theatre	Scritture with some control or influence	Scritture without control

1714
*Rodomonto
sdegnato*
car, S. Ang.
L: G. Braccioli
(ded. Vivaldi)
Music: M.A.
Gasparini

Orlando finto pazzo
aut, S. Ang. (10.11.)
L: G. Braccioli
(ded.)
M: 2

Orlando furioso
aut, S. Ang. (1.12.)
L: G. Braccioli
(new ded.)
Music:
Ristori + Vivaldi

1715
Nerone fatto Cesare
car, S. Ang.
L: M. Noris
(+ Braccioli?)
Music: Pasticcio
M: 3 – Brescia, car.

Lucio Papirio
car, S. Ang.
L: A. Salvi
(ded. Vivaldi)
Music: L.A. Predieri

1716 *Arsilda regina di Ponto* aut, S. Ang. L: D. Lalli (ded. anon!)	1716 *La costanza* ... car, S. Moisè L: A. Marchi (ded.) M: 4 *Arsilda, Regina di Ponto,* Venice 1716, aut. M: 6 [M: 7 *Juditha triumphans*]

I Full opera seasons with control of theatre	II One-opera seasons with control of theatre	III Scritture with some control or influence	IV Scritture without control
1717 *Penelope la casta* car, S. Ang. (opera 2ª) L: M. Noris – ? Music: F. Chelleri *L'incoronazione di Dario* car, S. Ang. (opera 3ª) L: A. Morselli – ? M: 5–1716, car. *Tieteberga* aut, S. Moisè L: A. Lucchini M: 8			
1718 *Armida al campo d'Egitto* car, S. Moisè (12.1.) L: G. Palazzi *Artabano rè dei Parti* (= 1716) car, S. Moisè L: A. Marchi (ded.) M: 9	**1718** *Armida al campo d'Egitto* pri, Mantua L: G. Palazzi (ded. P. Ramponi) M: 10 (M: 44, Venice 1731, car.)	**1718** *Scanderbeg* est, Pergola Florence L: A. Salvi M: 11	
1719 *Teuzzone* car, Mantua L: A. Zeno – ? (ded. G.A. Mauro) Music: (with arias by Orlandini?) M: 12 *Tito Manlio* car, Mantua L: M. Noris – (ded. Ingegnere del teatro)	**1719** *Artabano ...* (= 1718) car, Vicenza L: A. Marchi (ded. impresario)		

I Full opera seasons with control of theatre	II One-opera seasons with control of theatre	III Scritture with some control or influence	IV Scritture without control
Music: Act III by Vivaldi M: 13			
1720 *Alessandro cognominato Severo* car, Mantua (opera 1ª] L: A. Zeno –? (ded. Ingegnere del teatro) Music: Pasticcio (F. Chelleri and others)			1720 *Tito Manlio* car, Pace Rome (opera 1ª) L: Noris – ? Music: Boni + Giorgi + Vivaldi M: 14 (M: 17, Mantua 1720)
1720 *La Candace* car, Mantua (opera 2ª) L: D. Lalli – ? (ded. anon.) M: 16	1720 *Gli inganni per vendetta* (= 1718) car (?),Vicenza T. Cestari) L: Palazzi M: 18		
La verità in cimento aut, S. Ang. L: G. Palazzi M: 15			
	1721 *La Silvia* est (28.8.), Milan L: E. Bissarri –? M: 20	1721 *Filippo rè di Macedonia* car, S. Ang. (opera 1ª?) L: D. Lalli (dedica) Music: G. Boniventi (I, II) + Vivaldi (III) M: 19	
		1723 *Ercole sul Termodonte* car, Capranica Rome (opera 2ª)	

I Full opera seasons with control of theatre	II One-opera seasons with control of theatre	III Scritture with some control or influence	IV Scritture without control
		L: Bussani – ? M: 22	
		1724 *La virtù trionfante* ... car, Capranica (opera 2ᵃ) L: F. Silvani –? (ded. Capranica) Music: B. Micheli + Vivaldi + N. Romaldo M: 24	
		Giustino car, Capranica (opera 2ᵃ) L: N. Beregan – P. Pariata – ? M: 25	
1725 *L'inganno trionfante* ... aut, S. Ang. L: Noris – Ruggieri (ded. A. Biscione) Music: Pasticcio arr. Vivaldi M: 28		1725 *La costanza trionfante* Mantua M: 29	1725 *L'Artabano* car, Mantua L: Marchi (ded. S. Burigotti) M: 26
1726 *Cunegonda* car, S. Ang. L: A. Piovene – ? Music: Pasticcio arr. Vivaldi? M: 31		1726 *La Tirannia castigata* Prague M: 30	
La fede tradita e vendicata car, S. Ang. L: F. Silvani – ? (ded. A. Biscione) M: 33 (M: 36 Bergamo, c. 1726)			

I	II	III	IV
Full opera seasons with control of theatre	One-opera seasons with control of theatre	Scritture with some control or influence	Scritture without control

Dorilla in Tempe
aut, S. Ang. (9.11.)
L: A.M. Lucchini
(ded.)
M: 35

1727
Medea e Giasone
car, S. Ang.
(opera 1a?)
L: G. Palazzi (ded.)
Music: G. F. Brusa

Farnace
car, S. Ang.
L: A.M. Lucchini
M: 32 (1726)

Farnace
(= 1727)
aut, S. Ang.
L: Lucchini

Orlando
aut, S. Ang.
L: Braccioli – ?

1727
Ipermestra
car, Pergola
Florence
(opera 2ª)
L: A. Salvi
M: 37 (1726)

Siroe rè di Persia
pri, Reggio Emilia
L: Metastasio (ded.:
Impresari)
M: 38

1728
Rosilena ed Oronta
car, S. Ang.
L: G. Palazzi (ded.
Impresario)
M: 39

*Gli odi delusi dal
sangue*
car, S. Ang (fine
carnevale)
L: A.M. Lucchini
Music: G.B.
Pescetti +
B. Galuppi

1729
L'Atenaide
car, Pergola Florence

I Full opera seasons with control of theatre	II One-opera seasons with control of theatre	III Scritture with some control or influence	IV Scritture without control
		L: Zeno – ? M: 40	
	1730 *Argippo* aut, T. Sporck, Prague L: Lalli – ? M: 42		1730 *Farnace* (= 1727) pri, T. Sporck, Prague L: Lucchini (perhaps without Vivaldi) M: 43
	1731 *Farnace* (= 1727) pri, T. Omodeo Pavia (4.5.) L: Lucchini M: 47	1731 *L'Odio vinto della costanza* car, Venice M: 45 (M: 74, car. 1739, Parma)	1731 *Alvilda regina dei Goti* pri, T. Sporck, Prague L: Zeno – ? Music: (without Vivaldi?) M: 41 Prague pri. 1730 (M: 48, Prague 1731) *Merope* aut, Graz Music: T. Albinoni + Vivaldi M: 46
1732 *Semiramide* car, Mantua (opera 1ª) L: F. Silvani – ? (ded. Impresario) M: 51 *Farnace* (= 1727) car, Mantua (opera 2ª) L: Lucchini (ded. Impresario) M: 52		1732 *La fida Ninfa* car, Verona L: S. Maffei (from 1730) M: 53 *Semiramide* Mantua M: 51	1732 *Doriclea* (= 1716) car, T. Sporck, Prague L: Marchi – ? (impr. Denzio) M: 50 (car.) *Dorilla in Tempe* (= 1726) pri, T. Sporck, Prague L: Lucchini M: 49 (pri.)

I Full opera seasons with control of theatre	II One-opera seasons with control of theatre	III Scritture with some control or influence	IV Scritture without control
1733 *Montezuma* aut, S. Ang. L: G. Giusti M: 55		1733 *Farnace* (= 1727) Florence M: 54	
1734 *Dorilla in Tempe* (= 1726) car, S. Ang. (opera 1ª?) L: Lucchini – ? M: 56 *L'Olimpiade* car, S. Ang. (opera 2ª?) L: Metastasio + Zeno (*Lucio Vero*) Music: Pasticcio arr. by Vivaldi M: 57			
1735 *Tamerlano (Bajazet)* car, Verona L: A. Piovene – ? (ded. Vivaldi) Music: Pasticcio arr. by Vivaldi M: 58 (M: 63: Verona, 1735) *Adelaide* car, Verona L: A. Salvi (ded. Vivaldi) M: 62 (M: 73, car. Graz, 1739 – *q.v.*)	1735 *Griselda* pri, S. Samuele L: Zeno – Goldoni (ded. anon.) M: 59		1735 *Il giorno felice* Vienna M: 64 *Aristide* aut, S. Samuele L: Goldoni (ded. Lalli) Music: not Vivaldi? Not in M.
		1736 *Ginevra principessa* *di Scozia* car, Pergola,	

180

I Full opera seasons with control of theatre	II One-opera seasons with control of theatre	III Scritture with some control or influence	IV Scritture without control
		Florence L: Salvi – ? M: 61 (Lucca, 1735)	
	1737 *Catone in Utica* pri, Verona L: Metastasio (ded. anon.) M: 67 (M: 70, Graz 1740, *q.v.*)		1737 *Demetrio* car, Ferrara (opera 1ª) L: Metastasio – ? (ded. anon.) Music: Hasse, arr. by Vivaldi M: 65 *Alessandro nell'Indie* car, Ferrara (opera 2ª) L: Metastasio – ? Music: Hasse, arr. by Vivaldi (Libretto not found) Not in M. *Farnace* (= 1727) Treviso M: 66
1738 *L'oracolo in Messenia* car, S. Ang. (opera 1ª) L: Zeno – ? M: 70 *Armida al campo d'Egitto* (= 1718) car, S. Ang. L: Palazzi (ded. anon.) Music: Pasticcio, arr. Vivaldi M: 69	1738 *Siroe rè di Persia* (= 1727) est, Ancona L: Metastasio – ? (ded. Impresari) Music: Pasticcio, arr. Vivaldi? M: 72		1738 *Orlando furioso* (= 1714) car, Bergamo M: 68

181

I Full opera seasons with control of theatre	II One-opera seasons with control of theatre	III Scritture with some control or influence	IV Scritture without control
Rosmira car, S. Ang. L: Stampiglia (ded. Vivaldi) Music: Pasticcio, arr. Vivaldi M: 71 (M: 75, aut, 1739 Graz)			
		1739 *Adelaide* car, Graz M: 73 *Rosmira* aut, Graz (with Anna Girò) M: 75 *Feraspe* aut, S. Ang. L: F. Silvani – ? (ded. G.F. Dini) Not in M.	1739 *Siroe rè di Persia* (= 1727) car, Ferrara (opera 1[a]) L: Metastasio – ? (ded. Impresario) (with Anna Girò) *Farnace* (= 1727) car, Ferrara (opera 2[a]) L: Lucchini – ? Not performed; replaced by: *Attalo re di Bitinia* (Music: Hasse) Not in M.
			1740 Car, Graz *Catone in Utica* (= 1737) (with Anna Girò) M: 77

APPENDIX II
Vivaldian Ritornello Form

Maverick though Vivaldi undoubtedly was, he was none the less an impeccable formalist. The classical Vivaldian ritornello form, as it is called, derives its name from the four (or more) times that the orchestral introduction, or ritornello, generally appears. As a scheme it looks like this in a work in a major key:

		Key Structure
Ritornello I	Orchestra	I (tonic)
Solo I	Soloist(s) and basso continuo	I – V (dominant)
Ritornello II	Orchestra	V
Solo II	Soloist(s) and basso	V – VI (submediant: minor key)
Ritornello III	Orchestra	VI
Solo III	Soloist(s) and basso continuo	VI – I (tonic)
Ritornello IV	Orchestra	generally a repetition of Ritornello I in the tonic

In minor key works, the modulation might function as follows (our example is from *L'estro armonico*, Opus 3, No. 8, for two solo violins and orchestra with basso continuo in A minor):

Ritornello I	Orchestra	I (tonic)
Solo I	Soloists with upper strings accompaniment	I – III (mediant, C major)
Ritornello II	Orchestra	VII – IV (sub-dominant, D. minor)
Solo II	Soloists (with upper strings acc.)	IV
Ritornello III	Orchestra	IV

Solo III	Soloists (with upper strings acc.)	IV – I
Ritornello IV	Orchestra	I (shortened)
Solo	Soloists (with upper strings acc.)	I
Ritornello V	Orchestra with soloists	I

This schematic listing does not, of course, indicate all the times when Vivaldi breaks the mould by inserting short orchestral sections into the solo sections and by inserting short solo sections into the ritornelli. And of course Vivaldi is too original to adhere rigidly to any fixed scheme, and like Mozart with his own piano concerto form, he varies the basic pattern whenever he is so minded.

APPENDIX III
Bach's Arrangements

It is amusing to see what Bach makes of the intensely violinistic passage in Opus 3, No. 10 (see p. 45), when he transcribes it for four harpsichords. First, he drops Vivaldi's orchestral accompaniment and gives this whole middle section – for the French Overture returns briefly to conclude the movement in a symmetric fashion – only to the four harpsichords, in the following fashion:

It is a model of how a transcription into a totally different medium can be almost as effective as the original, provided that one has the mind, heart and understanding of Johann Sebastian Bach.

APPENDIX IV
Vivaldi's Published Collections

In Vivaldi's lifetime, the following sets of works were published:

OPUS	TITLE	NO. OF WORKS	PUBLISHER	PLATE NO.	DATE
3	*L'Estro Armonico*	12 concertos	Estienne Roger	50–1	1711
4	*La Stravaganza*	12 concertos	Estienne Roger	399–400	c.1712
5	*Sonate/Quatro à Violino Solo e Basso*	6 violin sonatas	Jeane Roger	418	1716
6	*VI Concerti/a Cinque Stromenti*	6 concertos	Jean Roger	452	1716–7
7	*Concerti/à Cinque Stromenti*	6 concertos	Jeanne Roger	470–1	1716–7
8	*Il Cimento dell' Armonia/e dell' Inventione/ Concerti/a 4 e 5*	12 concertos	Michele Carlo Le Cène	520–1	1725
9	*La Cetra/Concerti*	12 concertos	” ”	533–4	1727
10	*VI Concerti/à Flauto Traverso*	6 flute concertos	” ”	544	1728
11	*Sei/Concerti*	6 concertos	” ”	545	1729
12	*Sei/Concerti*	6 concertos	” ”	546	1729
13	*Il Pastor Fido,/ Sonates,/pour/la Musette, Viele, Flûte, Hautbois, Violon/avec la Basse continüe*	6 sonatas	Paris/chez Mr Boivin	—	1737

OPUS	TITLE	NO. OF WORKS	PUBLISHER	PLATE NO.	DATE
[14]	VI/*Sonates*/ *Violoncello Solo*/ *con Basso*	6 cello sonatas	Paris/chez M^r. le Clerk le cadet (ann. *Mercure de France.* Dec. 1740, p. 2919)		

The two preceding *opera* were, respectively, string trios and violin sonatas published, as we have seen, in Venice on old-fashioned movable type, as follows:

1	*Suonate da Camera/a tre/Due Violini e Violone o Cembalo*		Venice, Sala, perhaps c. 1703, reprinted (?) by Sala c. 1705; republished by Estienne Roger, Amsterdam, pl. no. 363
2	*Sonata/A Violino, e Basso per il Cembalo*		Venice, Antonio Bortoli MDCCIX 1709; republished by Estienne Roger, Amsterdam, pl. no. 2; both in score (a rarity in those days).

APPENDIX V

Kolneder on the Uffenbach Cadenza

❧

The Dresden autograph bears the remark 'Fatto per la Solemnita della S. Lingua di S. Antonio in Padua' (Composed for the Feast of the Holy Tongue of St. Antonio in Padua) and is generally dated as 1712. In the third movement, seven bars before the end, is the direction 'Qui si Ferma à piacim:' (Here there is a pause ad libitum), then the cadenza prescribed by it is written out. From the second note of bar 25 on, the composer has inserted a square bracket under the stave which extends as far as the 4th bar before the end. It follows from analogous uses of such brackets and from the two linking passages that this is clearly to be read as an octave transposition upwards. However, this means that as early as 1712, when Locatelli was only seventeen, Vivaldi was using the 12th position. The highest note of this cadenza, the F-sharp'''', however, already lay beyond the fingerboard of the so-called short-necked violins (or rather, violins of the old measure) played in Vivaldi's time. Thus it would seem that Vivaldi had had a longer fingerboard fitted for his own use. If Uffenbach's report is compared with this cadenza, it can even be assumed that at the opera performance in question the Concerto [RV 212 (Pincherle, 165)] with the written-out cadenza, was played: the imitations could refer to the motivic working, and the indication 'on all four strings' perhaps refers to the still relatively rare use of the G string in the double stopping of the tenth bar. But just as astonishing as the technical acumen of this cadenza is the compositional expertise: it begins in 4/4 time, although the third movement is in 3/4 time. The change back to 3/4 comes after 19 bars, but a few bars later, the 4/4 is taken up again and continues to the end of the cadenza. The orchestra's closing ritornello is once more in the time signature of the whole movement, 3/4. This change of beat was necessary because the composer made use of motivic material from the first movement, which is in 4/4 .... Vivaldi used a similar, though simpler procedure in the [Concerto in C for 2 violins RV 507 (Pincherle, 23)]. With these, Vivaldi wrote the first so-called 'cyclical' cadenzas, in other words, cadenzas which rework motivic material from all three movements of the cyclic form.

APPENDIX VI
Vivaldi's Church Music

Talbot's division of the church music into three periods has been followed: I (1713–7); II (c.1720–35); III (1739)

MASSES

Mass and Sections of the Mass Sacrum (RV 586)
Contemporary MS in the University Lib. Warsaw: authenticity not assured: no other source has been located.

1   Kyrie in G minor a due cori (RV 587) Talbot II
(a) score, etc, Ricordi (Degrada); (b) miniature score, Philharmonia 903
(Füssl)   Autograph in Turin
4/4 Adagio – Allegro – Adagio – Allegro

2   Gloria in D (RV 588), with Introduzione 'Jubilate, o amoeni chori' (RV 639a)
score, etc., Carus-Verlag (H. Bögel) – Talbot I.
Autograph in Turin.

i	Gloria	3/4 Allegro	Chorus	D major
ii	Et in terra pax	4/4 Largo	Chorus	B minor
iii	Laudamus te	3/8 Allegro	Duet for 2 sopranos & orch.	G major
iv	Gratias agimus	4/4 Adagio	Chorus	E minor
v	Domine Deus	4/4 Largo	Contralto solo & orch.	E minor
vi	Domine, Fili Unigenite	¢ Andante	Chorus	F major
vii	Domine Deus, Agnus Dei	2/4 Allegro	Solo oboe & contralto solo with Orch.	A minor
viii	Qui tollis peccata mundi	4/4 Adagio	Chorus	A minor
ix	Qui sedes	3/8 Largo	Contralto solo & orch.	
x	Quoniam tu solus sanctus	4/4 Allegro	Sop. solo & orch.	D major
xi	Cum Sancto Spiritu	4/4 – ¢ Adagio – Allegro	Chorus	D major

3   Gloria in D (RV 589) Scoring: oboe, trumpet, strings and continuo with SATB choir and soloists (Malipiero)   Talbot I
Score, etc. Ricordi (Malipiero) Autograph in Turin

The scheme of the movements, very similar to RV 588, is as follows:

189

i	Gloria	4/4 Allegro	Chorus	D major
ii	Et in terra pax hominibus	3/4 Andante	Chorus	B minor
iii	Laudamus te	2/4 Allegro	two Sops.	G major
iv	Gratias agimus	4/4 Adagio	Chorus	E minor
v	Propter magnam	₵ Allegro	Chorus	E minor
vi	Domine Deus	12/8 Largo	Sop. Solo (oboe or violin solo)	C major
vii	Domine, Fili Unigenite	3/4 Allegro	Chorus	F major
viii	Domine Deus, Agnus Dei	4/4 Adagio	Contralto solo & chorus	D minor
ix	Qui tollis peccata mundi	4/4 Adagio	Chorus	A minor
x	Qui sedes	3/8 Allegro	Alto solo	B minor
xi	Quoniam tu solus sanctus	4/4 Allegro	Chorus (as Gloria shortened)	D major
xii	Cum Sancto Spiritu	₵ Allegro	Chorus	D major

4   Credo in E minor (RV 591) for Choir (SATB) and strings with basso continuo (organ). There are no soloists. Talbot I

Autograph in Turin. (a) score, etc. Ricordi (Malipiero); (b) score, miniature score, etc, Universal Edition (Fasano).

4(a)   Credo in G (RV 592) Talbot I

Contemporary MS. in the University Lib. Warsaw: authenticity not assured; no other source has been located.

PSALMS, etc.

5   Dixit Dominus in D (RV 594) Psalm 109 (Vulgate) a due cori with preceding Motet (Introduzione) Talbot II
(see also under motet 'Canta in prato' (RV 623))
Both autographs in Turin
5(a)   Dixit Dominus in D (RV 595) Contemporary MS. in National Museum Prague: authenticity not assured; no other source has been located. Talbot I

Scores
(1)   Canta in prato – Ricordi (Talbot);
(2)   Dixit – Ricordi (Malipiero).
Scoring ('Canta in prato') – soprano solo, strings, continuo (organ). Dixit's scoring: 2 oboes, 2 trumpets, two orchestras with strings, bassi continui (organs), two SATB choirs and soloists: two sopranos, A-T-B. A third trumpet part in Coro II. When in movement VII, the trumpet in Coro II is used, the musician could leave his post in Coro I beforehand and return there afterwards.

As noted above, this was probably not written, at least in this state, for performance at the Pietà.

i	Dixit Dominus	4/4 Allegro	
ii	Donec ponam inimos tuos	4/4 Largo	
iii	Virgam virtutis tuae	4/4 Allegro	Duet for two sopranos (coro I, coro II) and two orchestras
iv	Tecum principium	3/4 Andante	Aria for contralto and orchestra (coro I)
v	Juravit Dominus	4/4 Adagio	Chorus (coro I, II)

vi	Dominus a dextris tuis	4/4 Allegro	Duet for tenor and bass with orchestra (coro I)
vii	Judicabit in nationibus	3/4 Largo – 4/4 Allegro molto	Coro I, II, strings, continui (organs)
viii	De torrente	4/4 Andante	Aria for soprano and orchestra (coro II)
ix	Gloria Patri	4/4 Allegro	Coro I, II – all forces
x	Sicut erat in principio	4/4 Allegro	Coro I, II – all forces (minus oboes, trumpets). Chorus

6   Beatus vir in C a due cori (RV 597). Psalm III. Talbot II. Autograph in Turin
Scoring: 2 oboes, strings, basso continuo (organ) SATB choir, soloists.
(a) Score, etc. Ricordi (B. Maderna); (b) score, etc. miniature score, Universal Edition, Philharmonia 906 (Fasano).

7   Beatus vir in B Flat (RV 598). Talbot I. Autograph in Turin.
Scoring: 2 solo sopranos, alto solo, SATB choir, strings, continuo (organ).
     This is a much shorter and less elaborate setting of Psalm 111 – possibly intended for the Pietà.

8   Laudate pueri in G (RV 601) for soprano, solo flute, two oboes and orchestra with basso continuo (organ). Talbot II. Autograph in Turin.
Score, etc. Ricordi (Ephrikian).

i	Laudate pueri	2/4 Allegro non molto	G major
ii	Sit nomen Domini	3/4 Allegro	E minor
iii	A solis ortu usque ad occasum	4/4 Andante	D major
iv	Excelsus super omnes	12/8 Larghetto	B minor
v	Suscitants a terra	3/8 Allegro molto	G major
vi	Ut collocet	2/4 Allegro	G major
vii	Gloria Patri	4/4 Larghetto	A minor
viii	Sicut erat in principio	2/4 Allegro (non molto)	G major
ix	Amen	3/8 Allegro	G major

9   Laudate pueri in A (RV 602) a due cori for two solo sopranos, chorus (SATB) and two orchestras with continuo (organ). Talbot I. Autograph in Turin
Score, etc. Carus-Verlag (F. Giegling). (Several other versions [RV 600, 602a, 603] [also in Turin]).

i	Laudate pueri	Allegro	Two solo sopranos, chorus and two orchestras
ii	A solis ortu usque ad occasum	Allegro	Soprano I, orchestra and continuo I
iii	Excelsus super omnes	Andante	Soprano II, orchestra and continuo II

iv	Quis sicut Dominus	Andante	Soprano I, orchestra and continuo I
v	Sit nomen Domini	Allegro	Chorus, 2 orchestras and continui
vi	Suscitans a terra	Allegro	Two soprano soli, 2 orchestras and continui
vii	Ut collocet	Allegro molto	Soprano II, orchestra and continuo II
viii	Sit nomen Domini	Allegro	Chorus, 2 orchestras and continui
ix	Gloria Patri	Andante	Soprano I solo, solo oboe and continuo I
x	Sicut erat in principio	Allegro	Solo sopranos I, II, chorus, 2 orchestras and continui

10   Laudate Dominum in D minor (RV 606), Psalm 116, for chorus, orchestra and continuo (organ). Talbot I. Autograph in Turin
Score,etc. Carus-Verlag (Giegling).

11   Laetatus sum in F (RV 607), Psalm 121, for chorus, string orchestra and continuo (organ), Talbot I. Autograph in Turin
Score, etc. Carus-Verlag (W. Horn).

Part of the Vespers for the feast day of the Virgin Mary. The elegantly simple chordal writing of the chorus is accompanied by Vivaldi's usually rhythmic string group.

12   Nisi Dominus in G minor (RV 608), Psalm 126, for contralto solo, string orchestra and basso continuo (organ). Talbot I (?) Autograph in Turin
Score, etc. (i) Ricordi (Degrada); (2) Universal Edition (Fasano).

i	Nisi Dominus	4/4 Allegro	G minor
ii	Vanum est vobis	3/4 Largo and 'Surgite' 4/4 (Presto, Largo)	B flat
iii	Cum dederit	12/8 Largo G minor	G minor
iv	Sicut sagittae	3/8 Allegro E flat	E flat
v	Beatus vir	4/4 Andante, leading to	B flat
vi	Gloria Patri	Larghetto	D minor
vii	Sicut erat	4/4 Allegro	G minor

13   Lauda Jerusalem in E minor a due cori (RV 609), Psalm 147. Two solo sopranos, two choruses and two string orchestras with continui (organs). Talbot I. Autograph in Turin
Miniature score: Eulenburg 1081 (J. Braun).

14   Magnificat in G minor (RV 610, other versions RV 610a, 610b, 611).
Score: (1) Ricordi, with 1739 additions (Malipiero): (2) Osek version, Universal Edition (Landon).

Scoring: strings, basso continuo (organ) SATB choir, soloists. Another version is for two cori. See below.

HYMNS, ANTIPHONS, etc

15   Salve Regina in C minor a due cori (RV 616) for contralto solo, two recorders, one flute, two string orchestras with continui (organs). Score, etc. Ricordi (Ephrikian), wherein the recorder and flute parts are fused as 'Flauto' I, II. Talbot II. Autograph in Turin.

i	Salve Regina	3/4 Andante	All forces (minus flute)
ii	Ad te clamamus	4/4 Allegro	All forces
iii	Ad te suspiramus	4/4 Larghetto	Contralto solo, one flute, Orchestra I, continuo I
iv	Eja ergo	2/4 Allegro	Contralto solo, orchestras I and II, continui I and II, without flute or recorders
v	Et Jesum	3/8 Andante molto	All forces except flute and recorders
vi	O clemens	3/8 Andante	All forces except flute

16   Stabat Mater in F minor (RV 621) for contralto solo, strings and basso continuo (organ). Talbot I. Autograph in Turin
Score, etc. Ricordi (Malipiero)

i	Stabat Mater	3/4 Largo	F minor
ii	Cujus animam	4/4 Adagissimo	C minor
iii	O quam tristis	3/8 Andante	F minor
iv	Quis est homo	3/4 Largo	F minor
v	Quis non posset	4/4 Adagissimo	C minor
vi	Pro peccatis	3/8 Andante	F minor
vii	Eia mater	4/4 Largo	F minor
viii	Fac ut ardeat	12/8 Lento	F minor
ix	Amen	3/8 Allegro	F minor

17   Motet 'Canto in Prato' in A major for soprano and orchestra with basso continuo (RV 623) – see Dixit Dominus (No. 5, supra). Talbot II.

18   Motet 'In furore giustissimae irae' in C minor (RV 626) for soprano and strings with basso continuo (organ). Talbot II. Autograph in Turin
Score, etc. Ricordi (P. Everett).

19   Motet 'In turbata mare irato' in G (RV 627) for soprano and strings with basso continuo (organ). Talbot II. (Authentic MS in Sächsische Landesbibliothek, Dresden, with autograph corr.)
Score, etc. Ricordi (Talbot).

20   Motet 'Invicti bellate' in G (RV 628) for soprano, strings and basso continuo (organ). Talbot I. Autograph in Turin
Score, etc. MS. (Ferenc Szekeres).

21   Motet 'Nulla in mundo pax sincera' in E (RV 630) for soprano, strings and basso continuo (organ). Talbot I. Autograph in Turin
Score, etc. Ricordi (Everett).

Notes on the Text

PROLOGUE

[1] *Ezra Pound and Music: The Complete Criticism*, edited with commentary by R. Murray Schafer. New York, 1977, p. 504.
[2] When I produced the first recording of the Bach transcription for the Haydn Society in 1949, it was difficult even in Vienna, where the recording was made, to organize four harpsichords.

CHAPTER 1

[1] Eleanor Selfridge-Field, p. 219. (For full bibliographical references, see Select Bibliography.)
[2] Remo Giazotto, pp. 11ff., translation by Michael Talbot; Talbot, p. 39.
[3] Walter Kolneder, p. 8; Talbot, p. 38.
[4] The mystery is that no one has yet discovered which Legrenzi work was the basis of Bach's adaptation. Malcolm Boyd: *Bach*, London 1983, p. 259.
[5] Francesco Caffi: *Storia della musica teatrale in Venezia* (MS. c. 1850); see Talbot, p. 40, n. 20.
[6] Kolneder, p. 8f., quotation p. 9.
[7] Giazotto, p. 285, n. 19.
[8] Pincherle, p. 17.
[9] Kolneder, p. 9.
[10] Talbot, p. 24.
[11] Giazotto, p. 352. English translation from Talbot, p. 42, who reminds us that 'viola' meant in those days violoncello rather than viola, which was usually referred to as 'violetta,' 'alto viola' or 'tenore viola.'
[12] Giazotto, p. 352. English translation in Talbot, p. 43. The 'viola all'inglese' is a kind of viola d'amore with six strings tuned D-G-c-e-a-d' and with sympathetic vibrating strings behind the bridge. Talbot, pp. 159f.
[13] Translation from Talbot, p. 45.
[14] Pincherle, pp. 24f; Talbot, pp. 19f.; de Brosses: Pincherle, p. 26.
[15] *Some Observations made in travelling through France, Italy, etc. in the Years 1720, 1721 and 1722*. 2 vols., London 1730, I, p. 99. Kendall, p. 16; Pincherle, p. 19.
[16] Kendall, p. 14.
[17] Kendall, p. 16; Pincherle, p. 19.
[18] Pincherle, p. 20.
[19] Giazotto, p. 93; translation by Talbot, p. 47.
[20] The original Italian *inter alia* in Giazotto, p. 292, n. for p. 90.

CHAPTER 2

[1] O.E. Deutsch: *Handel, A Documentary Biography*, London 1954, p. 27.
[2] Giazotto, pp. 96f.
[3] Giazotto, p. 102.
[4] *Ibid.*
[5] Pincherle, pp. 40f.; Talbot, p. 57.
[6] Giazotto, pp. 102–5.
[7] C. Freschot: *Nouvelle rélation de Venise*, 3 vols. in 1, Utrecht 1709, p. 318. Kendall, p. 17.
[8] Talbot, p. 49 (translation). Italian originals, Giazotto 1973, p. 365, and for lists of new works required pp. 363f.
[9] Walter Kolneder: 'Vivaldis "Brutszeit" als Opernkomponist,' in *Antonio Vivaldi: Teatro Musicale, Cultura e Società*,' ed. Lorenzo Bianconi & Giovanni Morelli, Florence 1982, 2 vols., I, pp. 229ff. Translation of 1710 document: Talbot, p. 50 (original in Giazotto 1973, p. 363f.) 2

June 1715: Giazotto 1973, p. 368. English translation: Talbot, pp. 50f.
[10] Giazotto 1973, p. 368. English translation in Talbot, pp. 50f. In other words, no one among the Pietà's governors minded their substitute *maestro di musica* having a double profession – as an opera composer and impresario, and as 'house composer' of church music for the Pietà.

CHAPTER 3

[1] Talbot, p. 54.
[2] Kolneder, pp. 95ff.
[3] O.E. Deutsch, *Handel*, pp. 487f.
[4] Malcolm Boyd: *Bach*, London 1983, pp. 148ff., 176.
[5] Kolneder, p. 39.
[6] ALLI DILETTANTI DI MUSICA, Il cortese compatimento, che sin'hora avete donato alle mie debolezze, m'ha persuaso a studiare di compiacervi con un'Opera de Concerti Istrumentali. Confesso ben che se per il passato le mie composizioni oltre i loro diffetti anno ancora avuto il discapito della stampa, hora il loro maggior avantaggio sara quello d'essere scolpite dalla mano famosa di Monsieur Estienne Roger. Quest'è una ragione per la quale ho studiato di sattisfarvi con la stampa de Concerti e mi fa corraggio di presto presentarvi un altra Muta de Concerti à 4. Conservatemi il vostro buon genio, e vivete felici..

CHAPTER 4

[1] Eberhard Preussner: *Die musikalischen Reisen des Herrn von Uffenbach*, Kassel etc., 1949, pp. 67 *passim*.
[2] Talbot, p. 57.
[3] Preussner, *op. cit.*, p. 67.
[4] Preussner, p. 71. English translation: Pincherle 1958, pp. 41f.
[5] Kendall, p. 57.
[6] John Julius Norwich: *Venice: The Greatness and the Fall* (vol. 2 of his Venice series, of which the first is *Venice: The Rise to Empire*), London 1981, pp. 321f.

This unexpected necessity of fighting on two fronts at once probably suggested to the Turkish commander that if he could not take Corfu quickly he would be unlikely to take it at all. On the night of 18 August he ordered a general assault, to the accompaniment, as always, of an ear-splitting din of drums, trumpets, rifle and cannon fire and hideous shrieks and war-cries – psychological warfare of a primitive but by no means ineffectual kind. [The Venetian commander, Marshal Mathias Johann von der] Schulenburg and his Proveditor-General Antonio Loredan were instantly at their posts, summoning every able-bodied Corfiot – women and children, the old and infirm, priests and monks alike – to the defences. After six hours the fighting was still desperate, with neither side gaining an obvious advantage; and Schulenburg decided to stake all on a sudden sortie. At the head of 800 picked men, he slipped out of a small postern and fell on the Turkish flank from the rear. The success was immediate – and decisive. The Turks were taken utterly by surprise and fled, leaving rifles and ammunition behind them, while their colleagues along other sections of the wall, bewildered and mystified, saw that the assault had failed and also retired, though in better order. The next night, as if to consolidate the Venetian triumph, a storm broke – a storm of such violence and fury that within hours the Turkish camp was reduced to a quagmire, the trenches turned to canals, the tents torn to ribbons or, their guy-ropes snapped like thread, lifted bodily into the air and carried off by the gale. In the roadstead, many of the Turkish ships, similarly driven from their moorings, crashed into each other, splintering like matchwood.

When dawn broke and the full extent of the damage was revealed, there were few indeed of the erstwhile besiegers who wished to remain another moment on an island where the very gods seemed to be against them; and indeed within a matter of days orders reached the Turkish camp to return at once. Corfu was saved; Schulenburg was awarded a jewelled sword, a life pension of 5,000 ducats, and the honour of a statue erected in his lifetime in the old fortress; and the Turks withdrew, never again to seek to enlarge their empire at the expense of Christian Europe.

[7] It is in the library of the Conservatorio di Santa Cecilia in Rome. The cast was:

Moyses	Barbara
Aaron	Candida
Elysabeth Aaron Uxor	Silvia
Maria soror Moysis et	Michielina
Aaron	
Pharao Egypti Rex	Anastasia
Sapiens primus	Soprana
Sapiens secundus	Meneghina
Unus ex Regis Ministris	Apollonia
Unus ex Ch. Ebraeor.	Gieltruda
Una ex Ch. Foeminar. Ebr.	Detta
Nuncias	Anna

(Elisabeth, Wife of Aaron; Maria, sister of Moses and Aaron; Pharaoh, King of Egypt; first wise man; second wise man; one of the ministers of the King; one of the chorus of Jews; one of the chorus of Jewish women; messenger.) [Kolneder, pp. 194f.]
[8] Leipzig 1767, pp. 285ff. The letter-spaced and bold-faced words have here been reproduced normally.
[9] Talbot, p. 65.
[10] Luigi Cataldi: 'Alcuni documenti relativi alla permanenza di Vivaldi a Mantova', in: *Informazioni e Studi Vivaldiani* 8 (1987), pp. 13–22.
[11] *Informazioni e Studi Vivaldiani* 8 (1987), pp. 19.
[12] Dated 3 March 1720. Claudo Gallico: 'Vivaldi dagli Archivi di Mantova', in: *Vivaldi Veneziano Europeo* (ed. F. Degrada), Florence 1980, pp. 77–88.

CHAPTER 5

[1] Vivaldi Concerto Manuscripts in Manchester in *Informazioni e Studi Vivaldiani* numbers 5, 6, 7 Milan (1984/5/6).

CHAPTER 6

[1] E. Selfridge-Field: 'Marcello, and *Il Teatro alla moda*' in *Antonio Vivaldi: Teatro Musicale, Cultura e Società* (ed. Lorenzo Bianconi and Giovanni Morelli), 2 vols., Florence 1982, II, 538.
[2] Talbot, p. 69.
[3] Giazotto, p. 119.
[4] Selfridge-Field, *op. cit.*, p. 544.
[5] Talbot, p. 70.
[6] Strohm, p. 48.

[7] Michael Talbot: 'Vivaldi's Serenatas: Long Cantatas or Short Operas' in *Antonio Vivaldi: Teatro Musicale, Cultura e Società* (ed. Lorenzo Bianconi and Giovanni Morelli), 2 vols., Florence 1982, I, 81f.
[8] Giazotti, p. 175.
[9] Talbot, 'Vivaldi's Serenatas', pp. 84ff.
[10] Selfridge-Field, 'Marcello, and *Il Teatro alla moda*', p. 535.
[11] Fabrizio Dell Seta: 'Documenti inediti su Vivaldi a Roma' in *Antonio Vivaldi: Teatro Musicale, Cultura e Società* (ed. Lorenzo Bianconi and Giovanni Morelli), 2 vols., Florence 1982, II, 521ff.
[12] 'Herrn Johann Joachim Quantzens Lebenslauf, von ihm selbst entworfen,' in F.W. Marpurg: *Historisch-Kritische Beyträge zur Aufnahme der Musik*, vol. 1, Berlin 1754–5.
[13] Talbot, p. 130.

CHAPTER 7

[1] 'Antonio Vivaldi compose due vespri?', *Nuova Rivista Musicale Italiana*, iii (1969) pp. 652ff.
[2] Talbot, p. 201. His new chronology: 'Vivaldi's Sacred Vocal Music: The Three Periods', in: *Nuovi Studi Vivaldiani, Edizione e cronologia critica delle opere* (ed. Antonio Fanna and Giovanni Morelli) vol. 2, Florence 1988, pp. 7859ff.
[3] *Ibid.*
[4] Programme booklet for the 1939 Siena performance. I must thank the staff of I Tatti in Florence for photographing all the material of this and the other early Chigi festivals.

CHAPTER 8

[1] Pincherle, pp. 22f., and Giazotto p. 191.
[2] Lino Moretti: 'Un cembalo per la Girò, *Informazioni e Studi Vivaldiani* 1980 (Ricordi), pp. 58ff.
[3] Giazotto, p. 191.
[4] Giazotto, p. 192.
[5] Giovanni Comisso: *Les agents secrets de Venise 1705–1797*, Paris 1990, pp. 23f.
[6] Giazotto, p. 261.
[7] *Scoperta e ricupero di musiche ... dei veneziani maestri*, p. 14.
[8] This information from the French version of Pincherle, pp. 218ff.
[9] 'Vivaldi and a French Ambassador', *Informazioni e studi Vivaldiani*, II, 1981, pp. 31–41 and 'Vivaldi's Serenatas' in

Antonio Vivaldi: Teatro Musicale, Cultura et Società (ed. Lorenzo Bianconi and Giovanni Morelli), 2 vols., Florence 1982, I, 82 ff and 92 ff.

[10] A manuscript 'relazione', discovered by Talbot, describes Vivaldi's part in the festivities as follows: 'The Serenata, which was a musical composition in praise of, and with good wishes for, the marriage of H. most Christian M., was given in the rooms of the loggia situated at the end of the garden, and was the composition of Signor Vivaldi, performed by most excellent musicians and singers; with their suave voices, these new Orfeos were posted in an infinite number of gondolas, which hide the very sea from the eyes of the spectators'. In the penultimate number, there is a direct reference to Languet, 'E voi, Signor, ch'in sen dell'Adria or fate / Questi degni sponsali / Con gioia festeggiar, io ne decoro / L'alto pensier . . .'.

[11] Giazotto 1973, p. 193.

[12] Giazotto, pp. 118, 196 f., 207f.

CHAPTER 9

[1] Giazotto, pp. 1206f.

[2] A discovery made by Michael Talbot: Talbot, pp. 77f.

[3] Österreichische Nationalbibliothek, S.m. 2452, Vivaldi's work on f. 58v. Talbot, 'Vivaldi's Serenatas', p. 80.

[4] Giazotto, pp. 210 ff.

[5] Rudolf Eller: 'Vier Briefe Antonio Vivaldis' in *Informazioni e Studi Vivaldiani* 10 (1989), pp. 5–21.

[6] Carlo Vitali: 'Vivaldi e il conte bolognese Sicinio Pepoli. Nuovi documenti sulle stagioni vivaldiane al Filarmonico di Verona' in: *Informazioni e Studi Vivaldiani* 10 (1989), pp. 25–39, esp. pp. 32, 34, n. 48 and 49.

[7] Pravoslav Kneidl: 'Libreta italské opery v Praze V 18 století. *Strahovska knihovna*, Prague 1966, pp. 97ff.; Talbot, pp. 78f.

[8] Talbot, p. 80.

[9] Giazotto, p. 221, 303.

[10] Published here from the facsimile in Talbot, p. 100ff.

[11] Giazotto, p. 199.

[12] Carlo Vitali, *op. cit* (see note 6 above), pp. 40–54, where all the documents are presented in facsimile and in transcription (the petition to the Academy has been produced many times, see n. 35, but here p. 54, for the first time in transcription). There is an extremely useful currency table, which we herewith reproduce from p. 55, an account book of 1715, wherein the currency is translated into lire and Bolognese soldi:

Doppia di Spagna o luigi		16-15
	di Roma	16-10
	Italia	16- 5
	nuovi	10- 5
Zecchin	———	
	vecchio	10-=
Ongaro et £9-5		9
Genoina		6-12
Filippo		4-16
Scudo, ducatoni tutti		10-10
Livaria [!]		9
Fiorin		4- 5
Ducato		3-10
Bianco vel Giulio		0-12
Scudo di Bologna		4
Madonnina		- 6

[13] A second instalment has just appeared in *Informazioni e Studi Vivaldiani* 12 (1991): C. Vitali: 'I fratelli Pepoli contro Vivaldi e Anna Girò', pp. 19–46, wherein we learn that Sicinio's eldest brother Alessandro was exiled from Venice for attempting to poison his wife. This charming little operation was opposed by Piero Pasqualigo, a great admirer (and perhaps more?) of Anna Giraud and a staunch supporter of Vivaldi and the 'old-fashioned' Venetian opera school.

CHAPTER 10

[1] Kendall, pp. 77ff.

[2] An English translation in H.C. Robbins Landon: *Chronicle and Works, Haydn at Eszterhaza 1766–1790*, London 1978, p. 412. Da Ponte's account in English translation: *Memoirs of Lorenzo Da Ponte*, translated by Elisabeth Abbott, Dover Publications, New York 1967, pp. 148ff. Extracts in H.C. Robbins Landon: *Mozart the Golden Years 1781–1791*, London 1989, pp. 155 *passim*.

[3] Translation from the English version of Pincherle, pp. 61f.

[4] Talbot, p. 83.

[5] Pincherle French, p. 24; English, p. 49. Giazotto, p. 222.

CHAPTER 11

[1] Giazotto: *passim*. Adriano Cavicchi: 'Inediti nell'epistolario Vivaldi-Bentivoglio' in: *Nuova Revista Musicale Italiana* 1 (1967), pp. 45–79. 'Fac simile et traductions de cinq nouvelles lettres de Vivaldi a Bentivoglio' in: *Vivaldiana* 1, Brussels 1969, pp. 117–41. Lino Moretti: 'Dopo l'insuccesso di Ferrara' in: *Vivaldi Veneziano Europeo*, pp. 89–99. Francesco Degrada: 'Le lettere di Antonio Vivaldi pubblicate da Federigo Stefani: un caso di "revisione" ottocentesca' in: *Informazioni* 5 (1984), pp. 83–9.

[2] Both operas by Vivaldi, for Florence (1736) and Venice (1734).

[3] Possibly Hasse's setting.

[4] In Sotheby's catalogue of its sale on 6 December 1991, in which this autograph letter appears as lot 25, the date is given as 26 November. But Vivaldi's '1' often appears to be '2' because of the way in which he writes (e.g. autograph letter of 10 June 1730, above, p. 114).

[5] Karl Heller, pp. 371ff. Adriano Cavicchi, 'Inediti nell'epistolario Vivaldi-Bentivoglio,' in: *Nuova Rivista Musicale Italiana* 1 (1967), pp. 45–79. Lino Moretti: 'Dopo l'insuccesso di Ferrara: Diverbio tra Vivaldi e Antonio Mauro', in: *Vivaldi Veneziano Europeo* (ed. F. Degrada). Florence 1980, pp. 89–99 (where the following documents are printed in the original Italian).

CHAPTER 12

[1] Giazotto, p. 262. See also Appendix I.

[2] Pincherle, French version, pp. 24f., including relevant Dutch references.

[3] Pincherle, French version, p. 25. Also for de Brosses *infra*.

[4] Giazotto, p. 248.

[5] Pincherle, French version, p. 26.

[6] Giazotto, p. 263; English in Talbot, p. 91.

[7] 'Un reçu autograph de Vivaldi daté de Vienne le 28 Juin 1741' in: *Vivaldiana 1* (1969) Brussels, p. 142: fac simile of document. Vivaldi is also mentioned in the diary of Duke Anton Ulrich von Sachsen-Meiningen, who was then in Vienna. Vivaldi was received once (7 February 1741) but refused on 8 and 11 February. Heller, pp. 344f.

[8] Pincherle, French version, p. 33; Kendall, p. 93.

[9] Gastone Vio: 'Alla ricerca delle date del'ultimo addio di Vivaldi a Venezia' in: *Informazioni e Studi Vivaldiani* 11 (1990). Graz in 1739.

[10] H.C. Robbins Landon: *Haydn, Chronicle and Works. The Early Years, 1732–1765*, London 1980, p. 58. The details of Vivaldi's death were first published by Rodolfo Gallo in *Ateneo Veneto*, fasc. xii (December 1938) and in 'L'atto di morte di Antonio Vivaldi' in *La scuola veneziana*, Siena 1941. The details are also in Walter Kolneder: 'Biographisches um Antonio Vivaldi', *Österreichische Musikzeitschrift* 1952, No. 2, pp. 54. The documents in the original read:

28 Dito (July 1741)
Der wohl Ehrwürdige Herr Antonj Vivaldi, welt. Priester im Satlerischen Hauss Beym Kartner Thor, in Spittaler Gottsacker. Klein gleuth.

(Wien, Dom- und Metropolitanpfarramt St. Stephan, Totenbuch, Tomo 23, Fol. 63).

Conduct Vivaldi
Den 28 July
Der wohl Ehrwürdige Herr Antonj Vivaldi, welt. Priester im Satlerisch. Haus beym Kartnerthor an Inneren brand bschaut worden, alt 60 Jahr, im Spitaller Gotsacker.

Kleingleüth	2:36
Herrn Curaten	3:–
Bahrtuch	2:15
Pfarrbild	–:30
Grabstell	2:–
Bahrleicher u. Mesner	1:15
Kirchendiener	–:30
6 Trager mit Mantl	4:30
6 Windlichter	2:–
6 Küttenbuben	–:54
Bahr	–:15
Pelicam	19:45

(Wien, Dom- und Metropolitanpfarramt St. Stephan, Totenbuch, Tomo 1741, Fol: 199)

Translation:
28th ditto [July 1741]
The most worthy Herr Antonj Vivaldi, Secular Priest, in the Saddler's House at the Kärtner Thor, in the Hospital Burial Ground. Pauper's bells.
[Vivaldi's funeral train;]
Train for Vivaldi:
The most [etc. repetition of above ...]
Kartnerthor, coroner's verdict: death from

internal inflammation, 60 years old, in Hospital Burial Ground

	(fl.)	(kr.)
Pauper's bells	2	36
Curates	3	–
Pall	2	15
Parish emblem	–	30
Burial site	2	–
Gravedigger & Sexton	1	15
Sacristan	–	30
6 Pallbearers	4	30
6 Storm lanterns	2	–
6 Choirboys	–	54
Bier	–	15
Pelicam [Total]	19	45

The poverty and anonymity are the same as in the recently discovered memorial service for Mozart on 10 December 1791, which cost twelve florins nine kreuzer. Document exhibited in the Mozart Memorial Exhibition (*Zaubertöne, Mozart in Wien*), 1990.

[11] Pincherle, French version, p. 27.

EPILOGUE

[1] On Durazzo see Robert Haas: *Gluck und Durazzo*, Vienna 1925. For Durazzo and Haydn, see H.C. Robbins Landon: *Haydn, Chronicle and Works, The Early Years 1732–1765*, London 1980, pp. 361 *passim*. On Durazzo, Vivaldi, etc.: Alan Kendall, pp. 101ff., Walter Kolneder, *Vivaldi: His Life and Work*, London 1970, pp. 2ff.

[2] Vivaldi studies have until about a decade ago lagged behind those for the more celebrated 18th-century composers, Bach, Handel, Haydn and Mozart. Recently, however, Vivaldi scholars have been producing an extraordinary series of articles on chronology and paper studies (watermarks, rastrology, etc.). Paul Everett's study, 'Towards a Vivaldi Chronology' in *Nuovi Studi Vivaldiani*, II, 1988, pp. 729ff., will undoubtedly lead to a whole new basis for Vivaldi research.

Select Bibliography

❧

A good bibliography is to be found in Karl Heller: *Antonio Vivaldi*, Leipzig 1991.

GIAZOTTO, Remo: *Vivaldi*. Milan 1965. Revised and amplified as: *Antonio Vivaldi*, Turin 1973. The standard work in Italian, valuable *inter alia* for its original research and the *verbatim* quotations of original sources.

HELLER, Karl; *Antonio Vivaldi*, Leipzig 1991. The latest and most sophisticated biography, utilizing all the latest sources.

KENDALL, Alan: *Vivaldi*, London 1978. Well illustrated and with useful sections on the historical and social background of Venice, this is a prettily written and useful survey.

KOLNEDER, Walter: *Antonio Vivaldi; Leben und Werk*, Wiesbaden 1965 (English translation as *Antonio Vivaldi: his life and work*, translated by Bill Hopkins, London 1970).

—— *Aufführungspraxis bei Vivaldi*, Leipzig 1955.

—— *Antonio Vivaldi, Dokumente seines Lebens und Schaffens*, Wilhelmshaven 1979 (2nd ed. 1983).

—— *Lübbes Vivaldi Lexikon*, Bergisch Gladbach, 1874.

Of immense erudition and with many insights into the form and performance of Vivaldi's music, these valuable books also include the authentic history of the great Turin Vivaldi MS. collection and how it came to the library.

OHMURA, Noriki: *A Reference Concordance Table of Vivaldi's Instrumental Works*, Kanagawa 1972. A useful concordance.

PINCHERLE, Marc: *Antonio Vivaldi et la musique instrumentale*, 2 vols., Paris 1948. The first great Vivaldi biography of our age, and still of great value. There is a facsimile of a long autograph letter which Pincherle owned. Seven years later he published an abridged version, *Vivaldi* (Paris, 1955), translated by Christopher Hatch as *Vivaldi: Genius of the Baroque*, New York 1957, London 1958.

RYOM, Peter: *Antonio Vivaldi – Table de Concordances des Oeuvres*, Copenhagen, 1973. Published in German as *Verzeichnis der Werke Antonio Vivaldis: Kleine Ausgabe* (Leipzig, 1974). This is the Ryom-Verzeichnis, by which Vivaldi's music is now identified (RV).

SELFRIDGE-FIELD, Eleanor: *Venetian Instrumental Music from Gabrieli to Vivaldi*, Oxford 1975. A very useful study.

STROHM, Reinhard: *Italianische Opernarien des Frühen Settecento (1720–1730)*, Cologne, 1976.

TALBOT, Michael: *Vivaldi*, London 1978. The standard work in English, full of insights.

Vivaldi, Periodicals and Reports

❧

Antonio Vivaldi da Venezia all'Europa, ed. Francesco Degrada e Maria Teresa Muraro, Milan 1978.

Vivaldi Informations, vols. 1 ff, 1972 (vol. 2, 1973, in expanded form).

Antonio Vivaldi: Teatro Musicale, Cultura e Società, 2 vols., ed. Lorenzo Bianconi and Giovanni Morelli, Florence 1982.

Informazioni e Studi Vivaldiani. Bollettino dell'Instituto Italiano Antonio Vivaldi, 1–11 (1980–1991).

Nuova Rivista Musicale Italiana. Antonio Vivaldi. Numero speciale in occasione del terzo contenario della nascità (1678–1978), January/March 1979.

Nuovi Studi Vivaldiani. Edizione e cronologia critica delle opere, ed. Antonio Fanna and Giovanni Morelli, 2 vols., Florence 1988.

Studien zur Aufführungspraxis und Interpretation von Instrumentalmusik des 18. Jahrhunderts, Heft 1–Heft 35, Blankenburg/Harz 1975–1988.

Venezia Vivaldi. Catalogue of the exhibition at S. Maria della Pietà, Riva degli Schiavoni, Venice, September–October 1978.

Vivaldiana 1. Publication du Centre International de Documentation Antonio Vivaldi, Bruxelles 1969.

Vivaldi Veneziano Europeo, ed. Francesco Degrada, Florence 1980.

Vivaldi-Studien. Referate des 3.Dresdner Vivaldi-Kolloquiums. Mit einem Katalog der Dresdner Vivaldi-Handschriften und Frühdrucke, Sächsische Landesbibliothek Dresden 1981.

Index

202

Index

Index

Index

SOURCES OF ILLUSTRATIONS

Bologna, Civico Museo Bibliographico Musicale 142 (top right); Chlumec Castle, Czech Republic 19, 138 (bottom), 139; Photo Costa 24; Ferrara, Archivio di Stato 144; Hamburger Kunsthalle 138 (top); Anthony Kersting 18 (bottom); London, Courtauld Institute of Art 22 (bottom); London, Mansell Collection 142 (top left); London, Sotheby's 172; Milan, Museo Teatrale alla Scala (photo Scala) 140 (left); Oxford University Music Department 142 (bottom right); Rome, Vatican Library 17; Venice, Cà Rezzonico (photo Scala) 23 (top); Venice, Casa Goldoni (Photo Osvaldo Böhm) 22 (top); Venice, Conservatorio di Musica 143 (all three); Venice, Fondazione Cini 141; Venice, Museo Correr (photo Osvaldo Böhm) 140–41; Venice, Pinacoteca Querini Stampalia (photo Scala) 23 (bottom).